# Prayers to Release You from Bondage, Recover You, and Make You Well in Jesus' Name

## Prayers for Healing

BELLANY JACKSON

WestBow Press books may be ordered through booksellers or by contacting:

WestBow Press
A Division of Thomas Nelson & Zondervan
1663 Liberty Drive
Bloomington, IN 47403
www.westbowpress.com
1 (866) 928-1240

Because of the dynamic nature of the Internet, any web addresses or links contained in this book may have changed since publication and may no longer be valid. The views expressed in this work are solely those of the author and do not necessarily reflect the views of the publisher, and the publisher hereby disclaims any responsibility for them.

Any people depicted in stock imagery provided by Thinkstock are models, and such images are being used for illustrative purposes only.
Certain stock imagery © Thinkstock.

Scripture taken from the King James Version of the Bible.

ISBN: 978-1-4908-7488-3 (sc)
ISBN: 978-1-4908-7489-0 (e)

Library of Congress Control Number: 2015904891

Print information available on the last page.

WestBow Press rev. date: 6/15/2015

First I must begin by thanking God for being God and sending His only begotton Son, Jesus Christ in whom we have Salvation through. I praise God for Jesus obedience, sacrifice, and love portrayed by the Word made flesh and dwelt among us. I praise God for Jesus teaching, healings, and unyielding saving power and that without the shedding of the blood of Jesus Christ there would be no remission of sin. I praise God for salvation, redemption, deliverance, wholeness, and safety, all found in Jesus Christ, where the fulness dwells which pleases His Father, God. I thank God that above all things, my desire is to please the Lord, for my name to be written in the Lamb's Book of Life, convert nonbeliever's to believer's in Jesus Christ, and to receive His abundantly overflowing blessings spiritually and financially. I praise God that demons are subject to the Word of God and that we should be holy and ready for Jesus Christ return. I pray this book will convert many to Jesus Christ and will deliver those oppressed, bring salvation to those in need of a Savior, and loose the bands of wickedness in high and low places, break every yoke, and undo heavy burdens in the name of Jesus Christ.

# Contents

Psalms 42:1
(To the chief Musician, Maschil, for the sons of Korah.) As the hart panteth after the water brooks, so panteth my soul after thee, O God.

Then hath no temptation taken you but such as is common to man: but God is faithful, who will not suffer you to be tempted above that ye are able; but will with the temptation also make a way to escape, that ye may be able to bear it.

1 corinthians 10 : 13

Isaiah 43:2
When thou passest through the waters, I will be with thee; and through the rivers, they shall not overflow thee: when thou walkest through the fire, thou shalt not be burned; neither shall the flame kindle upon thee.

BJP

KJB

# Jesus Christ Defeated All My Enemies

## Luke 10:19

Behold, I
give unto
you power to
tread on
serpents and
scorpions
and over all
the power of
the enemy
and nothing
shall by any
means hurt
you.

**KJB**

Made it through the waters,
Only because Jesus was with me,
Which did not overflow thee,
God is faithful
Who will not suffer you to be tempted
Above that you are able
And I still stand today choosing
To lie down in the green pastures
He maketh for thee, maketh for me
Without burns or flames kindling upon me
Because the Lord made a way of escape
Securing my ability to bear it through Him, Jesus
Who is head of all principalities and power
Who holds all power in heaven and in earth,
Who is the sacrificial lamb without blemish or spot
Because God is Love and it pleases Him
That the fulness dwell in Jesus Christ
Whom I love, trust, and depend daily
On my Lord and Savior Jesus Christ
Which healeth thee, healeth me
I am healed in Jesus name
Restored, Elevated, and
Have Overcome my Enemies
Only Through The Power of God and Jesus Christ
Praise the Lord!
I am healed in the name above every name

## I Peter 1:19

19 But with the precious blood of Christ, as of a lamb without blemish and without spot:
20 Who verily was foreordained before the foundation of the world, but was manifest in these last times for you,
21 Who by him do believe in God, that raised him up from the dead, and gave him glory; that your faith and hope might be in God.

## Jesus

by Bellany Jane Jackson
Poem Written 0912.2014

**Praise the Lord**

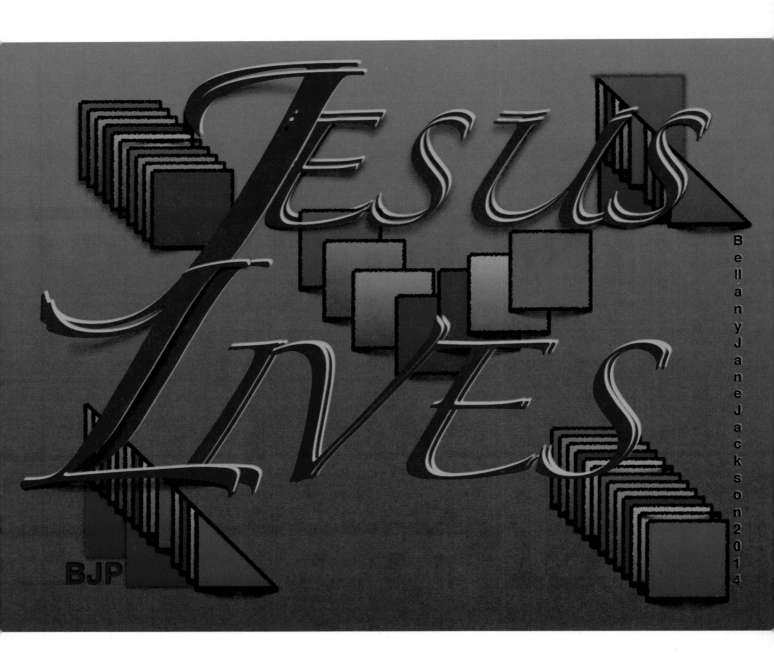

Acts 13:30 But God raised him from the dead:

I Peter 1:21 Who by him do believe in God, that raised up from the dead, and gave him glory; that your faith and hope might be in God

Galatians 1:1 Paul, an apostle, (not of men, neither by man, but by Jesus Christ, and God the Father, who raised him from the dead;)

Ephesians 1:20, Which he wrought in Christ, when he raised him from the dead, and set him at his own right hand in the heavenly places,

21 Far above all principality, and power, and might, and dominion, and every name that is named, not only in this world, but also in that which is to come:

Acts 3:15 And killed the Prince of life, whom God hath raised from the dead; whereof we are witnesses.

Romans 6:9 Knowing that Christ being raised from the dead dieth no more; death hath no more dominion over him.

Colossians 2:12 Buried with him in baptism, wherein also ye are risen with him through the faith of the operation of God, who hath raised him from the dead.

## Prayer for Roots of Hate

Father God in the Name of Jesus Christ
We ask you Lord
To saturate every root of hate
With the precious blood of Jesus Christ
And expose the enemy and his devices
Hate Known and Unknown
Hate Visible and Invisible
Hate displayed by a sheep in wolves clothing
Hate that is Family Related
Hate that is Non-Family Related
Hate stemmed through jealousy
Hate within the body of Christ
Hatred toward other races
Hate which will cause one not to forgive
Hate if left in that state will cause physical illness
Hatred in every Infected area
Lord send Jesus Christ in a stone-raining manner
Whom is sharper than any two edged sword
To deal with hearts disguised and visible
Lord deal with the hands, arms, legs, and feet of those eager to do mischief
Lord we thank you for replacing the hate with love
Lord we thank you for spoiling deceitful spirits
And that an honest holy spirit is now present
Lord we thank you for holding all power in Heaven and in Earth
Those things we failed to mention in the prayer
We ask the Holy Spirit to make intercession for us in the name of Jesus
In the Mighty Name of Jesus Christ our Lord and Savior

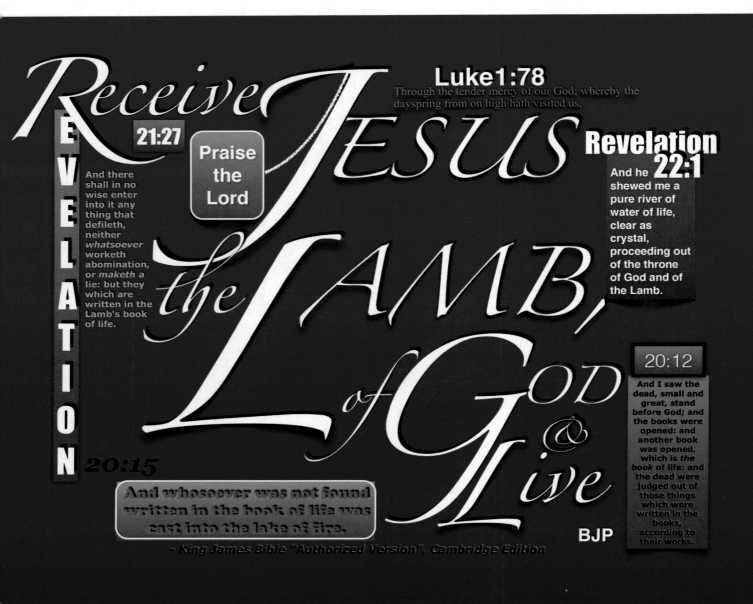

Receive JESUS the LAMB, of GOD & Live

**Luke 1:78**
Through the tender mercy of our God; whereby the dayspring from on high hath visited us,

**REVELATION**

**21:27**
And there shall in no wise enter into it any thing that defileth, neither *whatsoever* worketh abomination, or *maketh* a lie: but they which are written in the Lamb's book of life.

**Praise the Lord**

**Revelation 22:1**
And he shewed me a pure river of water of life, clear as crystal, proceeding out of the throne of God and of the Lamb.

**20:12**
And I saw the dead, small and great, stand before God; and the books were opened: and another book was opened, which is *the book* of life: and the dead were judged out of those things which were written in the books, according to their works.

**20:15**
And whosoever was not found written in the book of life was cast into the lake of fire.

- King James Bible "Authorized Version", Cambridge Edition

BJP

## Prayer for Overcoming the Enemy

Father God in the Name of Jesus Christ
Thank You for Bringing Down
King Og and the King Og's in My Life
And every other unrecognizable
Force of the enemy
Lord, Thank you for Psalms 18:17
You have delivered me
From my Strong Enemies
From them which hated me
For they were too Strong for me
Great is the Lord and greatly to be praised
For His greatness is unsearchable
I praise you because you dwell on the inside of me
And Greater is He that is within me
Than He that is in the world
I praise you because the Word of God tells me
That He overcame them by the blood of the Lamb
And the Word of His testimony
I praise you because you Lord
Are the Head of All Principality and Power
I praise you because there is one Lord and one Faith
One Baptism, One God and Father of All
Who is above all and through all and in you all

## Prayer for Court Room Justice

Father God in the Name of Jesus Christ
Lord you are above the courts
Allow your Holy Presence to Fill
Court Rooms Knowing You Lord
Are Head of all Principalities and Powers
Lord we ask you to restrain
Every wicked hand no matter the location
Make them subject
To your Mighty Right Hand
Knowing you Lord are our High Priest
In the Mighty Name of Jesus Christ
Our Lord and Savior

## Prayer for Education

Father God in the name of Jesus Christ
We ask you to fill the schools with your presence
We ask you to send your Holy Angels
To Combat Evil, Inequality, and Injustice.
We pray for compensation
For those whose education
Was cut short and careers struck.
We pray the Hand of God to Move
In our Favor
In the Mighty Name of Jesus Christ

## Prayer for the Word of God to Go Forth

Father God in the Name of Jesus Christ
Loose the Restraints placed
That dictate what may be preached
From the Word of God
The bible states let every man
Be a liar and the Word of God be true
Sin is Sin and God Hates Sin
Jesus Christ is the Perfect Example
Left for man to follow
That's why Holy Scripture
Which all inspired by God
Profitable for doctrine
For reproof, correction, and instruction in righteousness.
Also by the leading of the Holy Spirit
In the Mighty Name of Jesus Christ

## Prayers for Hospitals

Father God in the Name of Jesus Christ
We ask your presence in the hospitals
Nursing homes, and all medical buildings
We ask you to bind Satan and
All of his devices that hinder the healing of those sick
Physically, mentally, and sicknesses unknown to me
Deal with those whom abuse the medical financial system
In the Mighty Name of Jesus Christ

## Prayer for Bullies in General

Father God in the Name of Jesus Christ
We ask you to deal
With bullies in General (physical and spiritual)
We ask you to deal with the parents and overseers
Especially those aware of their behavior

We ask you to make the proper adjustments in the brain that control temper, anger, and the pleasure center. Lord regulate the dopamine levels and all others that contribute to these behaviors. Destroy the demonic forces working behind the scene, afflict them, and render them helpless in the name of Jesus Christ. Thank you in advance for healing the children and dealing with the parents. In the Mighty name of Jesus Christ, Our Lord and Savior.

## Prayer to Break the Spirit of Witchcraft

Father God in the Name of Jesus Christ
We ask you to bind
The spirit of witchcraft and every evil work
In places known and unknown in the name of Jesus Christ
The one's confessing a relationship with you with this in their hand.
We ask for the arrest of them and hold them bondage. Especially those who knew better indeed. No release until you Lord See Fit In the Name of Jesus.
Lord you said in the Word of God that witchcraft is an abomination and knowing this, we know it stinks in your nostrils. The Word of God said, "Is not this the fast that I have chosen to break every yoke, loose the bands of wickedness, undo heavy burdens, and set the oppressed free." Turn your plate, pray without ceasing, be holy for He is Holy and watch God. God is a discerner of all things and knows the intent of the heart and knows how, when, and what needs to be circumcised or cut by Jesus Christ, the sharper than any two edged sword, from the heart, joints, spirit, and marrow.

## Prayer to Bind Nursing, Medical, and other Unknown Wickedness

Father God in the Name of Jesus

We ask you to deal with agency wickedness, nursing wickedness at large, medical wickedness, and unknown wickedness unlimited hindering employment. Lord I ask you to move your mighty right hand and breathe on this situation. Lord we ask you to expose the evil and the breakdown in the systems. We ask you if necessary to move those whom refuse to comply out of the way in the Mighty Name of Jesus Christ. Lord we exalt and bless your Holy name in Jesus name.

## Prayer for the Bereaved Families Indeed

Father God in the Name of Jesus Christ

Lord it has been identified that during bereavement the minds of the loved ones are most sensitive. Sometimes they misconstrue those with genuine concern. Our prayer to identify to the bereaved those that care and are coming to support out of love and/or concern. We thank you that families will no longer mistreat those that really care. We ask you Lord to restrain the hands of the wicked in Jesus Name. Lord, we bind the release of things that would intentionally injury, cause malfunction, and contrariness to the Word of God.

## Prayer for the Healing of Minds

Father God in the Name of Jesus Christ

Lord we thank you for being God and thank you for the Word of God which states that "He whose mind is stayed on you, you will keep in perfect peace. **Proverbs 19:15, Slothfulness casteth into a deep sleep; and an idle soul shall suffer hunger.** Allow each individual to stay full with the Word of God by reading, studying, and hearing the Word of God. I thank you for breaking brass, cutting iron, and using of the shield of faith to quench all the fiery darts of the enemy. Allow us to continue being holy and in right standing with you Lord knowing you will block the devices of the enemy that may try to invade my mind and hinder my work. I thank you for the helmet of salvation in which I place this piece of armor daily along with my feet shod with the preparation of the gospel of peace. Jesus is the Prince of Peace. I pray for the presence of Jesus Christ to rest upon you and keep your minds in peace, perfect peace. Lord we ask for a continuous flow of the Word of God through our minds in the name of Jesus Christ. Lord those approaching and have past sixties, Lord we ask you to keep their minds intact and not allow the enemy to feed discord, trash, and filth to their minds, but allow them to be mindful of the scriptures, hymns, and psalms of praise with the ability to communicate effectively in all areas in the name of Jesus Christ. Lord heal the minds of all people, in all locations, all over the world in Jesus Mighty name.

## Prayer for the Conversion of Sinners to Jesus Christ

Father God in the Name of Jesus Christ for every tool the church is holding and practicing that the world uses. We ask you to save and convert rulers of the Darkness of this world to Jesus Christ to be honest sheep that hear your voice. Obedient to you Lord. They too will win souls to Jesus Christ in the Name of Jesus Christ.

# Jesus Christ

**MATTHEW**                    **4 : 23 - 24**

And Jesus went about all Galilee, teaching in their synagogues, and preaching the gospel of the kingdom, and healing all manner of sickness and all manner of disease among the people.

And his fame went throughout all **Syria**: and they brought unto him all sick people that were taken with divers diseases and torments, and those which were possessed with devils, and those which were lunatick, and those that had the palsy; and he healed them.

BJP                                  KJB                                  HJN

## Prayer for Deliverance from Sexual Sins

Father God in the Name of Jesus Christ. Lord, we ask you to deal with sexual sins that defile the body. Lord we ask you to wash eyes and mouths with the precious blood of Jesus Christ. We ask you to fill every sexual area with the blood of Jesus Christ in the Name of Jesus. Lord, we ask you to heal them and bring them back to line up with the Word of God. How you placed Adam and Eve in the garden and Noah and His Wife and three sons with their three wives on the ark. Lord we thank you in advance for protecting all ages in the Mighty Name of Jesus Christ. Lord you said in the Word of God after one has come into the knowledge of the truth that they should walk therein. Lord we ask for those that have been exposed to the truth to line up with the Word of God in the name of Jesus. Lord our goal is to see you one day knowing our names must be written in the Lamb's Book of Life. Lord allow us to do things that are pleasing in your site and will produce a sweet smelling savor in the name of Jesus Christ in your nostrils. Lord our ultimate goal is to praise you and live lives that will win souls to you and are pleasing in your sight. Lord allow us to resist the devil knowing he will flee from us in the name of Jesus Christ.

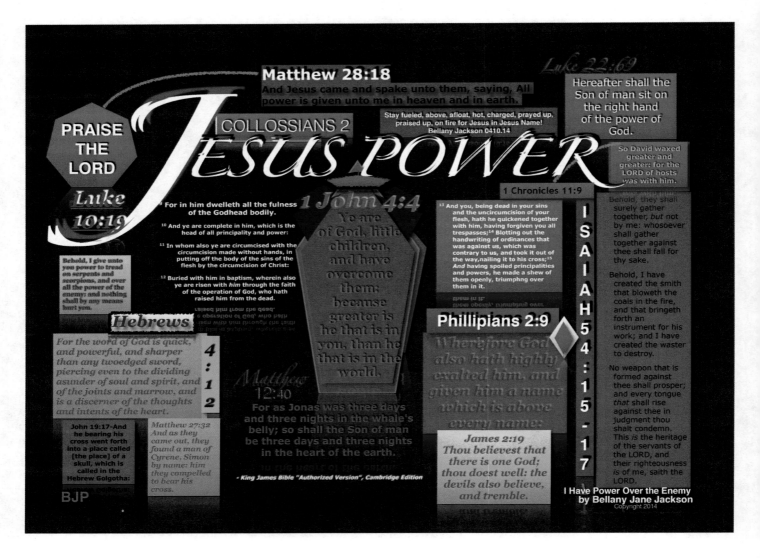

**I Have Power Over the Enemy**
**by Bellany Jane Jackson**
Copyright 2014

Praying Knowing the Power of God

Isaiah 54:16-17
**I created the smith that bloweth the coals in the fire that bringeth forth an instrument for his work and I have created the waster to destroy.**
**No weapon that is formed against thee shall prosper and every tongue that shall rise against thee in judgment thou shalt condemn for this is the heritage of the servants of the Lord whose righteousness is of me.**

God made Satan to destroy. God made Satan to destroy. **Proverbs 16:4, "The Lord hath made all things for himself: yea, even the wicked for the day of evil.** God made Satan to destroy. God is greater than all. God sent Jesus whom is life to give you life through the blood of Jesus Christ. Live, by staying connected to Jesus the true vine, which is the highway of holiness, the narrow road that leads to heaven. Jesus said "**I am the way the truth and the life, no man comes to the Father but by me.**" We must go through Jesus. We must believe Jesus. We must receive Jesus. We must allow Him, Jesus to dwell on the inside of us and believe in the Power of God and the Power of Jesus Christ. **Colossians 1:15-17, "Who is the image of the invisible God, the firstborn of every creature: For by him were all things created, that are in heaven, and that are in earth, visible and invisible, whether they be thrones, or dominions, or principalities, or powers: all things were created by him, and for him: And he is before all things and by him all things consist. Revelations 4:11, "Thou art worthy, O Lord, to receive glory and honour and power:**

for thou hast created all things, and for thy pleasure they are and were created." Ephesians 6:12 For we wrestle not against flesh and blood, but against principalities, against powers, against the rulers of the darkness of this world, against spiritual wickedness in high places. Finally know these Matthew 28:18, "And Jesus came and spake unto them, saying, All power is given unto me in heaven and in earth. Colossians 2:9-10, "For in him dwelleth all the fulness of the Godhead bodily. And ye are complete in him, which is the head of all principality and power." Revelation 12:11, "And they overcame him by the blood of the Lamb and the words of their testimony; and they loved not their lives unto the death."

## Prayer to Reveal our Enemies

Father God in the Name of Jesus Christ

Lord we ask you to identify to a true loved one those that are trying to promote, aid, and assist in their death. We ask if the behavior continues that you will afflict them of your choice Lord in the name of Jesus Christ.

9

## Prayer for Protection from the Enemy

Father God in the Name of Jesus Christ. I thank you that I am under God's surveillance system and nothing is missed, goes unnoticed, all recorded in heaven with the inability to be altered by the enemy. The Word of God states in **II Corinthians 5:10, Man shall give an account for every deed; whether it be good or evil.** I pray for protection in the sky, clouds, under the ground, trains, buses, airports, stations, beaches, and protection from those whom illegally walked in, have received passports to enter into the U.S, and have been granted citizenship whom try to harm, injure those whom were born here and brought here and freed. Lord we ask you to expose the enemy and his devices in the name of Jesus Christ. I pray for protection from known and unknown wickedness worldwide and spiritual wickedness in high and low places attempting to harm, injure, and cause danger, I pray for protection from spirits of others that desire to harm, we ask you to bind the ability for the enemy to transmit forces in environments that we occupy. We ask you to suffocate the enemy in these situations in the name of Jesus Christ. Lord protect homes from the enemy, protect saints of God indeed, whom have loved and served you and have been faithful to you, from attacks from the enemy in the name of Jesus Christ. I serve God and Jesus Christ in whom holds all power in heaven and earth and is head of all principalities and powers in the name of Jesus Christ. Lord we praise you for the Word of God, which will always stand. Lord in the name of Jesus, allow us to keep on as stated in **Ephesians 6:11 "Put on the whole armour of God that we will be able to stand against the wiles of the devil. Ephesians 6:13-17, Wherefore take unto you the whole armour of God, that ye may be able to withstand in the evil day, and having done all, to stand. Stand therefore, having your loins girt about with truth, and having on the breastplate of righteousness; And your feet shod with the preparation of the gospel of peace; Above all, taking the shield of faith, wherewith ye shall be able to quench all the fiery darts of the wicked. And take the helmet of salvation, and the sword of the Spirit, which is the word of God.** Lord you are the only one whom is able to keep me from falling in the name of Jesus Christ.

**Jude 1:24 Now unto him that is able to keep you from falling, and to present you faultless before the presence of his glory with exceeding joy, To the only wise God our Savior, be glory and majesty, dominion and power, both now and ever. Amen.**

## Prayer for Hospitals

Father God in the Name of Jesus Christ. We bind hospital wickedness in high and low places in the Name of Jesus. Lord we ask you to deal with wicked workers in high, low, and middle places in the name of Jesus. Lord we ask you to soften their hearts to you Jesus before you send your wrath in the Mighty Name of Jesus Christ. **John 3:36 states "He that believeth on the Son hath everlasting life: and he that believeth not the Son shall not see life; but the wrath of God abideth on him.** Destroy yokes, destroy fetters, loose bands of wickedness, bind the release of lust demons, and demons at large in the name of Jesus. Suffocate devices of the wicked, brattle the tongues and hands of the enemy in the workplace that their wicked agenda is ground to powder, knowing God has already overcome the enemy by the blood of Jesus Christ and Jesus is risen and alive, sitting on the right hand of His Father, God. Demonic beams the Lord rebuke in the name of Jesus Christ and the sender of them in the name of Jesus Christ.

## Prayer of Thanks to the Lord for Restraining our Enemies

Father God in the name of Jesus Christ. Thank you for restraining the hands of the enemy and detonating his devices and grinding them to powder those known and unknown to me in the name of Jesus Christ. Lord we thank you for your strong right hand. Thank you for being my God and sending our Savior and Lord, Jesus Christ. Thank you for pushing back walls that pushed in on me in the name of Jesus Christ

# Father GOD In the Name of JESUS CHRIST

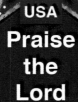

**USA**
**Praise the Lord**

Lord We Ask You In the Mighty Name of Jesus Christ
For Unlimited Surveillance
From You Lord and the Heavenly Angels &
Continue to Strengthen the United States Military
As They Both Protect The United States
Lord You Are Our Ultimate Protection
However, We Ask For
Those That Don't Know You
Will Surrender Their Lives To You
Lord We Ask You To Heighten
The Intelligence in the United States
Even More Due to the Breach
Thank You For Those Chosen To Protect Us
Knowing Lord You Are Above All
Thank You For Your Heavenly Surveillance System
Lord, We Worship and Praise You
Lord Give Those In Combat and on Assignments
an Unmeasured Amount of Strength According to Their Need
In the Mighty Name of Jesus
Thank You For Souls Won to You
and Additional Protection
Continue to Console Those Who Have Lost Loved Ones in Combat
and/or In the Line of Duty and Heal Those Injured
In the Mighty and Holy Name of Jesus Christ

0131.14BJJ

BJP

# JOHN 3:16

**SON OF GOD**

FOR GOD SO LOVED THE WORLD
THAT HE GAVE HIS ONLY BEGOTTEN SON
THAT WHOSOEVER BELIEVETH IN HIM
SHOULD NOT PERISH
BUT HAVE EVERLASTING LIFE
KJV

BLOOD
OF JESUS
= LIFE

BJJ

## Prayer to Stay Holy

Be Ye Holy, for I am Holy
Jesus was born holy and pure
We were born in sin
Molded in iniquity
Holiness is obtained through Jesus Christ
We have to put it on
When we accept Jesus in our Lives
He, Jesus
Began shedding off of us
The old man or sin
Putting on us the new man
Jesus Christ, the Word of God
Things your hands used to do
Places your feet used to take you
No longer takes place
Because Jesus has changed you
Thank God for Jesus Christ
Thank God for the Power in the Precious Blood of Jesus
Be Holy In Jesus Mighty Name.

## Prayer to Bind Hospital Wickedness

Father God in the name of Jesus Christ. Lord we ask you to bind hospital wickedness in the high and low places in the name of Jesus Christ. Lord we ask you to deal with wicked workers in high and low places and in between. Lord we ask you to deal with wicked families, patients, and staff in the name of Jesus Christ. Allow your Mighty hand Lord and our shield of faith to shield, combat, and destroy the ability of evil yokes to enter to cause havoc in the work place. Lord allow the hospital to be a place of physical, mental, social, emotional, and every type of healing needed in the name of Jesus to get people back on the right road to Salvation, the strait gate, the narrow road, the highway to righteousness, and back to the only mediator between God and men, the man Jesus Christ. Lord, we thank you for your Mighty hands of protection in the name of Jesus Christ. Lord we ask you to soften their hearts to you Jesus before you send your wrath in the Mighty Name of Jesus Christ.

## Prayer of Thanks to the Lord for Restraining our Enemies

Father God in the name of Jesus Christ. Thank you for restraining the hands of the enemy, detonating his devices, and grinding them to powder. Those known and unknown to me in the name of Jesus Christ. Thank you for your strong right hand. Thank you for being my God and sending our Savior and Lord, Jesus Christ. Thank you for pushing back walls that pushed in on me in the name of Jesus Christ.

## Prayer for Protection of Children

Father God in the Name of Jesus Christ

Protect children everywhere from evil visible and invisible. We ask the release of your Holy angels to expose locations of the missing and abducted everywhere. Heal their minds, protect them, and place them in an abuse free, loving, godly environment in the name of Jesus Christ. Allow them to overcome the enemy by your precious, holy blood shed and knowing you spoiled all principalities and powers shown in their lives by the ability to live normal lives depending, praising, worshipping, and honoring you Lord in the name of Jesus Christ. Lord correct problems with parents and children in general in the name of Jesus Christ. If they fail to take heed. We ask you to expose them in the Mighty name of Jesus Christ.

## Praise the Lord!

Daniel from the tribe of Judah
In a Foreign Land
Still praised and prayed to the only one God, the Living God
Now the only mediator between God and Men is Jesus Christ, the Lion of the Tribe of Judah. Wherever you go, take Jesus Christ with you. Going to college, take Jesus with you to class, the dorm, etc....
Moving to another state, take Jesus with you
Praise the Lord wherever you go
King David said, I will sing praises before the gods
Because there is one God and one mediator between God and Men, Jesus Christ

## Prayer for the States' Capitals

Father God in the Name of Jesus Christ
The Word of God states in Psalms 99:5 KJV, "Exalt ye the Lord Our God and Worship at his footstool; for He is Holy."
Lord, we ask your presence in the States Capitals
Lord send your sharper than any two edged sword,
Jesus Christ, the Word of God
To the very core of the root of evil
Seen and unseen

Visible and invisible
Known and unknown
Knowing all things Lord are visible in your eyes
To sever, abort, crush, cast into the sea
Satan and his weapons

Loose these bands of wickedness and break every yoke that suppress the people whom love, worship, praise, and are being holy as instructed in the Word of God. Lord we thank you in advance in the Mighty and Holy name of Jesus Christ, Our Lord and Savior in Jesus Name we pray.

## Praise the Lord

When God's long suffering for King Manasseh ended
He was bound in chains and fetters
Captured and suppressed until he cried out to God
**All stories don't' end like this**
Every evil and high place built before bondage
He brought down
When God released him
Your choice
Either you can ask God for assistance or he will do it when his time is right
II Kings 21 and II Chronicles 33 KJV

## Prayer for US troops in Afghanistan

Father God in the name of Jesus Christ
Look on Afghanistan and surrounding areas
Lord, Have your Holy angels
Combat the enemy and his devices
Thank you for our heavenly
Surveillance system that protect us at all times

## Prayer for Securing the Border

Father God in the name of Jesus Christ
Thank you for making every unsecured border secure
Thank you for making every place
Proclaiming the name of Jesus Christ Godly in the name of Jesus Christ
Thank you for making every Spirit of confusion
Subject to sound doctrine
Thank you for making every lying spirit
Be truthful in the name of Jesus Christ
Thank you for being my God
Thank you for sending Jesus the Christ
Thank you Lord for safety in the United States Through Jesus Christ
In Jesus Holy and Mighty Name

## Exalt Jesus Christ and Never Bow to the Beast

**Revelation 14:9** states, "And the third angel followed them, saying with a loud voice, if any man worship the beast and his image, and receive his mark in his forehead, or in his hand

Revelations 14:10 states, "The same shall drink of the wine of the wrath of God, which is poured out with mixture into the cup of his indignation; and he shall be tormented with fire and brimstone in the presence of the holy angels, and in the presence of the Lamb: KJV

## Our Prayer to Exalt Jesus Christ and Never Bow to the Beast

Father God in the name of Jesus Christ
Allow all those who know you Lord
And have a relationship and commune with you

With the connection to the True Vine, Jesus Christ, be so strong that they are inseparable. The True Vine and Branch like an eternal ball and socket joint. They will endure until the end like the Apostle Paul endured much suffering, tests, perils and trials but he left on record how the Lord continued to deliver him until it was time for him to depart the life in the flesh body. Apostle Paul went through perils of this and that but the Lord continued to deliver, like Daniel and the Hebrew Boys. We will continue to pray and not bow down, knowing you are able to deliver us from the fire in Jesus Holy and Mighty Name.

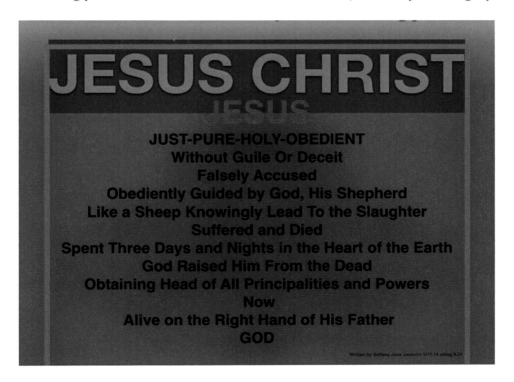

## Jesus Christ Obedience

Jesus was obedient even in suffering
Suffered like no other and died
He went down right and he got up right
Resurrected by God from the dead
Plan God designed accomplished
Right hand of the Father
Now He sits, Alive

## Prayer During Fasting

Father God in the name of Jesus Christ
As I turn my plate
I ask you to loose the bands of wickedness
Break every yoke
Set the oppressed free
Undo every heavy burden
According to Isaiah 58:6 in the name of Jesus Christ
I ask you Lord
According to Psalms 107:16
Lord thank you for cutting the bars of iron asunder
And breaking the gates of brass
I believe it is done
In the mighty and holy name of Jesus Christ

## Prayer to Bind Political Wickedness

Father God in the name of Jesus Christ
Lord we ask you to look upon political wickedness in high and low places and in between in the name of Jesus Christ. Look on and act on seen and unseen, known and unknown places to man in the name of Jesus Christ. During campaigns and after the elections in the mighty name of Jesus Christ, worldwide but especially in the United States of America. Lord we ask you to deal with the discord, hiding demons and others that attempt to halter aide for those in need and all those that attempt to hinder God's plan for our needs being supplied according to his riches in glory by the Lord our Shepherd. We ask the Lord to deal with those out of order and causing confusion. Lord, if they refuse to comply we ask your mighty hand to move, moving some out, not limited to all accountable for the confusion. In the Mighty name of Jesus Christ.

## Prayer to Expose Scams in the Name of Jesus Christ

Father God in the name of Jesus Christ,
Lord we ask you to expose of all scams unlimited
Regardless of route, mail, telephone, appointment, job offer, lies, and all others.
We ask you to correct and make it good and if noncompliant, then shut the operation down without compensation
To the Deceiver of the brethren, lying spirits
Used to distract, cause loss, and hinder the people of God
Whom proclaim they are connected to the true vine, Jesus
Lord deal with them first
If they refuse to submit to you
Lord we ask for exposure and/or removal in the name of Jesus Christ
Then Lord deal with those whom do not know you and convert them to Christians whom will walk in the truth and be holy and be a Holy Light
Whose life will win souls to Jesus Christ
Allow us, your people to be about your Kingdom business
Restoring souls, preaching the gospel to the poor
Healing the broken hearted, setting at liberty the captives
Just as you were in the mighty name of Jesus Christ
Through the Powerful name above all names, Jesus
**Neither is there salvation in any other**

For there is none other name under heaven given among men
Whereby we must be saved." Acts 4:12
Jesus, Head of all principalities and powers when God raised Jesus from the dead
Sent by our compassionate, loving, undefeatable, and triumphant living God.

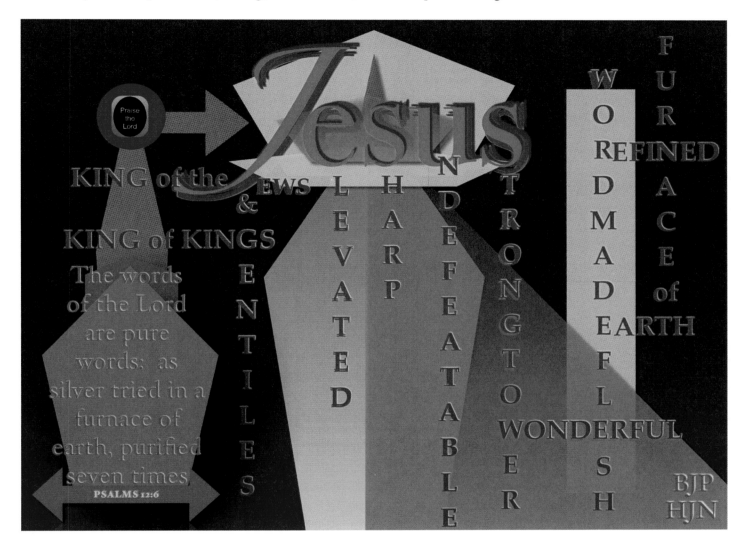

The Lord worthy of all the honour, glory, and power. And one that "Freely gave" His only begotten Son, Jesus, who said he would freely give to us all as well. **Romans 8:32 He that spared not his own Son, but delivered him up for us all, how shall he not with him also freely give us all things?** Let us win souls, pray, show love, compassion and let our God continue to provide abundantly for us. Jesus said in **John 10:10b, I am come that they might have life, and that they might have it more abundantly. Philippians 4:19, But my God shall supply all your need according to his riches in glory by Christ Jesus.**

Prayer to Keep the Commandments Which the Word of God States Are Not Grevious
FATHER GOD IN THE NAME OF JESUS CHRIST
The Word of God states **in John 15:10 KJV, "If ye keep my commandments Ye shall abide in my love. "Even as I have kept my Father's commandments and abide in his love. For this is the love of God that we keep his commandments and his commandments are not grievous," according to I John 5:3 KJV.** Our Prayer in the name of Jesus. Allow us Lord to keep your commandments and walk in the truth.

Continue to teach and perfect our love for others and Lord restrain the hands of those that desire our demise in the name of Jesus Christ. **Jeremiah 29:11 states, "For I know the thoughts I think toward you, saith the Lord, thoughts of peace, and not of evil, to give you an expected end."** We must understand, we too must have good thoughts for ourselves and thoughts that line up with the Word of God. **II Peter 3:9 states, "The Lord is not slack concerning his promise, as some men count slackness; but is longsuffering to us-ward, not willing that any should perish, but that all should come to repentance."** Are you aligning your life with the Word of God to ensure that your name is written in the Lamb's book of Life and that demons are subject to you. Lord thank you for consoling us with **Romans 3:24-25 stating, "For I am persuaded, that neither death nor life, nor angels, nor principalities, nor powers, nor things present, nor things to come, nor height, nor depth, nor any other creature, shall be able to separate me from the Love of God, which is in Christ Jesus Our Lord." Ephesians 4:5-6, states that there is "One Lord, One Faith, and One Baptism. One God and one Father of all, who is above all and through all and in you all."**

## Prayer to Deal with Drug Wickedness at Large Excluding No Areas

FATHER GOD IN THE NAME OF JESUS CHRIST
We ask you to deal with drug dealers, manufacturers, and distributers at Large.
Drug wickedness and abuse in the hospitals, businesses, and all places.
On the street, in the air, on and under the oceans, trains, and globally.

Police wickedness, gang violence and wickedness, ocean wickedness at large, authority wickedness at large, courtroom wickedness at large, and all other wicked areas. We ask you to send your Holy precious blood and Holy angels to combat areas known and unknown, visible and invisible, which all are subject to you Lord. Saturate starting at the root with the righteous blood of Jesus Christ. Lord, we ensure the holding of our shield of faith to quench every fiery dart of the enemy in the name of Jesus Christ. From the most veteran first to the newly joined in the name of Jesus. Abort the plan of the enemy and his devices in every area. We thank you Lord that you have given us power over the enemy and we stand on **Revelations 12:11, And they overcame him by the blood of the Lamb, and by the Word of His testimony; and they loved not their lives unto the death.** Knowing when God raised Jesus Christ from the dead, Head of all Principalities and Powers was accomplished. Knowing Lord, you hold these, we confidently with assurance, without reservation place these in your hands and cast all our care upon you Lord. The all powerful, all knowing, all seeing, and all sufficient God whom we believe will conquer the areas all mentioned and areas omitted and unknown in prayer. Thank you for converting many to Jesus Christ that will be sold out to you Lord in the name of Jesus Christ. Lord we thank you in the Holy, Righteous, Pure, Loving, and Compassionate name of Jesus Christ, the Shepherd and Bishop of our Souls and Lion of the Tribe of Judah's Mighty Name. In Jesus Name we pray.

## Prayer for the U.S. President, First Lady, and Family

Father God in the Name of Jesus Christ
**Cover the President** of the United States of America, Barack Obama with your precious blood and the First Family. Lord we thank you for Him and the Fear of the Only Living God that rest within Him in Jesus name. We ask your assistance with suppressing the enemy and his devices in the name of Jesus Christ. Every stronghold, yoke, spiritual wickedness in High and Low places, tea party agenda, and past wickedness unlimited, we ask you to suppress and destroy in the name of Jesus Christ. Lord previous presidential wickedness the Lord rebuke that hinder his ability to actively fulfill the role of President as elected. Look on every part of government and Religion and allow your presence to be present in the name of Jesus Christ that assist the President of the United States of America and others. Expose and deal with the counterfeit members of Government with intentions to harm openly or with deceit. Where the

breakdown in communication is found, if still present, we ask you to correct and mend each department per chain established to reach the President. The ones that continue in ways not of you Lord, we ask for you to deal with them not limited to moving them out of the way. For those that openly disrespect the first black President of the United States in His second term, regardless of color, we ask you to deal with them in the name of Jesus Christ. We thank the Lord that we, the United States, **Love Jerusalem (Psalms 122:6) and Pray for Peace** knowing "**they shall prosper that love thee.**" We thank you, pray maintenance, and an increase of respect for the Highest Office as President in the presence of the US, all nations, and before you Lord. Thank you for President Obama being the "Head of State and Government of the United States, who leads executive branch and federal government, and commander and chief of the US Armed Forces, and command authority over the largest active nuclear arsenal" and more whom God has chosen, Obama to be President at this time (Retrieved from http://en.wikipedia.org/wiki/President_of_the_United_States).

We ask for one accordness as close as achievable in the Mighty name of Jesus Christ.

Thank you for his wife and children and mother in law, and brothers. Continue to allow the United States First Lady Michelle Obama to be sensitive to his needs and any other omitted areas in the name of Jesus Christ. Be intuitive of intentional traps set up dealing with parties in government and outside government at all times in the name of Jesus Christ. Continue to protect them and shield them. Lord I ask they will never denounce you Lord, the Only Living God, Israel's God. Just as Daniel and the three Hebrew Boys would not stop praying to the only Living God, the God of Abraham, Isaac, and would not bow to idols. We will not bow to any of these including the beast as noted in Revelations, which will result in the wrath of God. Thank you for the "United States capital where the first black memorial achieved in 2011" where the August 28, 1963, "I Have a Dream" speech occurred on Capital Hill by Dr. Martin Luther King Jr. and Now in Honor of the First Non-elected black President in which God was with him. A memorial constructed of "white pure granite sculpted by a sculpterist from China." Dr. MLK, a light alive shined with life at five foot seven and now in honor of the light and of his life, "a standing statue thirty feet tall in the National Mall" commemorating his life, use of the weapons given in scripture to fight, and the "I Have A Dream" speech on Capital Hill (http://en.wikipedia.org/wiki/Martin_Luther_King,_Jr._Memorial). Perils of, perils of, perils of, but each time God delivered and now the US have reached the wealthy place in Jesus Name fulfilling more of the dream. He spoke about freedom, which was the goal for the black race and for all. Whose wife, family, fraternity brothers, civil rights activists and a host of others hold fast the memories of his life, legacy, and untouchable achievements and accolades. Dr. Martin Luther King Jr. also has a stone lying in honor of him in Israel, in which he loved the "Stone that the Builders Rejected" which is now the head stone of the corner, Jesus Christ, the King of the Jews and Gentiles. Rosa Parks bronze Statue Reside at the Statutory Hall of the U.S. capital on this 100th Anniversary unveiled on February 27, 2013 (http://www.whitehouse.gov/blog/2013/02/27/rosa-parks-has-permanent-seat-us-capitol.) Rosa Parks also has a Memorial building thirteen stories high in downtown San Bernardino (http://en.wikipedia.org/wiki/Rosa_Parks_Memorial_Building). Thank you for the Founding Fathers all previous Presidents, and those in Office, but everything dead allow it stay buried. Jesus Christ is the only one whom is risen from the dead, and alive, sitting on the right hand of His Father, God. Lord at times allow the consciousness of past occurrence that has happened in the Office remain afresh knowing, "There is One God and One Mediator between God and Men, the man Christ Jesus." Lord we ask in the name of Jesus Christ to keep them safe and in fine tune with the Holy Spirit and the will of God for the Country. Allow the President to maneuver around things that will distract and attempt to take away from his Presidency in the name of Jesus Christ. We thank you for President Obama, our First African American President of the United States of America, holding the Highest Office under oath.

## Prayer for Marriages Between a Man and a Woman Producing Fruit

Father God in the Name of Jesus Christ

We ask you look on families, in which you love. Marriages between a man and woman with offspring fulfilling **Genesis 1:28 "And God blessed them, and God said unto them, Be fruitful, and multiply, and replenish the earth, and subdue it: and have dominion over the fish of the sea, and over the fowl of the air, and over every living thing that moveth upon the earth."** We ask you to restore marriages that the enemy like a bulldozer was allowed to pull, pick, dig up, until the life of the marriage appeared to be gone. Lord you are a restorer. Just as a bulldozer is able to tear down a building, a bulldozer is able to bring fresh dirt to those involved to begin rebuilding a house. You have restored souls in people that appeared in the eyes of man was no hope. Lord, you restored life to bodies of many whom was diagnosed with terminal illnesses and given a death sentence, but today they have a testimony of how you restored, saved, healed, delivered them from the desire of the enemy. **Proverbs 18:21, "Death and life are in the power of the tongue: and they that love it shall eat the fruit thereof."** I choose to speak life in Jesus name. Like holding on to a seam in which the hem is out, therefore just loose strings, but now faith is the substance of things hoped for and the evidence of things not seen. Faith without works is dead. Have faith in God, Jesus said. In every situation God knows the intent of the heart, before you act, God knew. Even during the marriage ceremony, God knows the intent of the heart and I'm reminded that vengeance is mine saith the Lord! Lord knowing you are head of all principalities and powers, hold all power in heaven and in earth, we give this to you Lord in the name of Jesus Christ.

## Prayer for Recovery from Alcohol Addiction

Father God in the Name of Jesus Christ

We ask you to take the taste of alcohol out of the mouths of those with addictions, misuse, and abuse to this substance or others in the name of Jesus Christ. Lord we ask you to destroy the yokes, loose the bands of wickedness, sever the stronghold of the substance and we chose you Lord as our stronghold in the name of Jesus Christ. Lord we ask you to place people in the lives of those that pray this prayer that will be examples of living without alcohol or other addictions and with testimonies of how you Lord have truly indeed delivered them. Lord we ask you to replace the taste and desire for alcohol and other abused substances with the Word of God and Godly things in the name of Jesus Christ with a desire for a closer walk and relationship with you in the name of Jesus.

## Prayer for Dream Crushers

Father God in the Name of Jesus Christ

Lord we exalt your Holy and Mighty Name in the Name of Jesus Christ. Lord, Great you are and greatly to be praised. Lord we exalt you and worship at your footstool because you are holy. Lord we ask you deal with those that attempt to break others spirits that are worshipping, serving you sincerely, and are truly servants of the Lord whose righteousness is of you. Lord we ask you to suffocate the demonic forces in the name of Jesus Christ that it is no longer functionable in the name of Jesus Christ. This prayer is not limited to those that desire to crush dreams and aspirations of others. Lord you are a God of order and God that has perfect timing. Lord we ask you in the name of Jesus to fulfill the desires of those that love, worship, have believed and received you, whom continues to live a consistent life seeking you first and the kingdom of God, knowing that you will not withhold any good thing from us, as you freely gave your only begotton Son, Jesus. God with us, was with us in the flesh when the fulness of time had come. God watched Jesus heal, deliver, set free, make whole, restore, relieve, and make straight ailments in people lives. God watched Jesus, His only begotton Son without sin, suffer, be whipped with many stripes, crucified on a tree and die. God watched Jesus after His death go into the heart of the earth three days and three nights until God himself raised Jesus from the dead, where He sits alive on the right side of the Father God in Heaven. The love of God, the love of Jesus, the love of them both for mankind and especially for those that love Him and our love for the sacrifice of God and the sacrifice of Jesus made by giving His life in obedience to his Father knowing He could at any point call for the angels to deliver him. Be ye holy for I am holy. Live according to the Word of God and seek God first. Keep your eyes on Him, as if you were walking on the water. Look to Jesus because He is our help. Jesus is the resurrection. Jesus has resurrecting power (Jesus is the Resurrection, https://itunes.apple.com/us/album/do-you-know-brass-breaker/id925094879)

## Prayer for Children from Broken Homes

Father God in the Name of Jesus Christ

Lord we ask you to help children whose homes are currently broken deal with the separation. Lord go with them to school, recess, other functions that the mother now has to be both parents. Lord protect the boys while they are in the men's restroom and all other areas that mom cannot go in with them. Keep their minds stayed on you Lord and increase their obedience to their mother to line up with the word of God in the name of Jesus. Lord you are our provider. Lord allow both parties to do and provide as mature adults knowing the law is for the lawless. No need for the law when the children are fed, clothed, and the roof, floor, all structures including heat and air, daily needs met, and transportation are secure, but when the lines of communication are broken and fatherly provisions are not made, "the law is for the lawless" I Timothy 1:9, in the name of Jesus Christ.

## Prayer to Deal With In-Law Wickedness

Father God in the Name of Jesus

Deal with in-law wickedness in the name of Jesus Christ. Deal with unreasonable and deceptive ones in the name of Jesus Christ. Lord, you are a discerner of the heart in the deep, dark crevices. You are a discerner and know the intents from close and far. Lord, we ask you to whom the above applies that you will deal with their hearts in the name of Jesus Christ before judgment comes in the name of Jesus Christ. It's almost like your saying I love the children but I don't like who had them. Staying in the scripture, you cannot have a relationship with God without having Jesus Christ. Jesus said no man can come to the Father but by me. Jesus is the only one in which we may receive salvation, the only foundation laid that was laid (I Corinthians 3:11), authorized (Matthew 28:18, Colossian 1:19), and ordained by God (Ephesians 2:10) when the fulness of time had come. I ask God in the name of Jesus Christ to loose the bands of wickedness, destroy yokes, strongholds, and suffocate satan and his devices in the name of Jesus Christ. Every division demon, the Lord rebuke you in the name of Jesus Christ. Lord allow your Holy Stones to fall in the name of Jesus Christ and grind to power the demonic forces in the name of Jesus Christ. Lord we bind the spirit of witchcraft and every wicked work in the name of Jesus Christ. Those who know you and are holding the world's or devils instruments deal with them first knowing these are things that God hates in the name of Jesus Christ.

## Prayers for Healing

Lord we ask you to heal those with heart irregularities and malfunctioning hearts. Lord first we would like to look on the spiritual side and see if there is unforgiveness, hatred, envy, and other ungodly things that may cause the malfunction of the heart. If these and other problems exist we ask you to allow them to cast their care upon you for you careth for them. We ask that they release the person, people, situation, company, and/or whatever the problem, to free them from further bodily damage. Lord we ask you to heal the situations that led to the hypertension, enlarged heart, valve dysfunction, and other unnamed illnesses, if indeed caused from failure to release a situation, a person, or sin, which led to stress, and then led to physical body malfunction. Lord if this is a trial or test thank you for trusting us with this situation in the name of Jesus. Lord, we stand on **I Peter 2:24, "Who his ownself, bare our sins, in his own body, on the tree that we being dead to sin shall live unto righteousness by whose stripes we were healed."** Lord we thank you for allowing them to seek medical attention before it was too late. In Holy Scripture Lazarus heart stopped and was dead four days and also the child whom Elisha prayed was dead too (II Kings 4:32-37) and by the power of God they woke up (John 12:9-12). The damsel, Jesus stated in the Word of God was just sleeping when he woke her up (Mark 5:35-43).

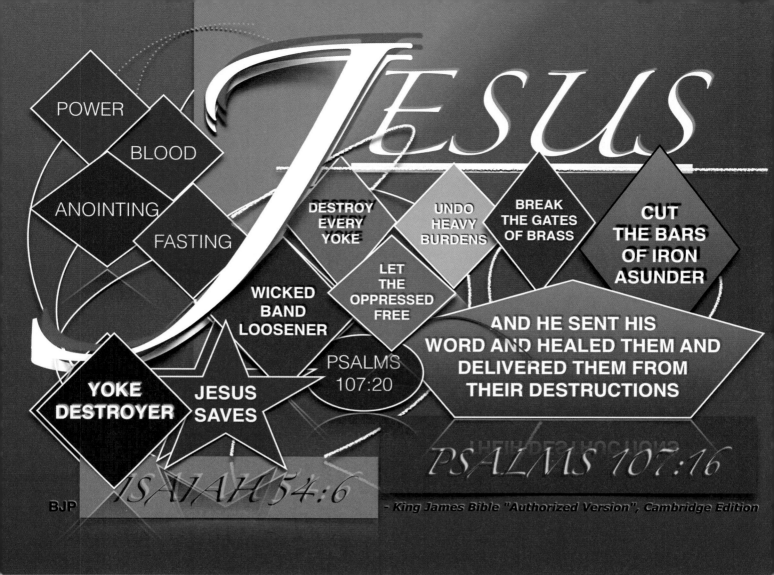

## Prayer to Deal With Spiritual Wickedness and Wickedness at Large

Father God in the Name of Jesus Christ

Lord, we ask you to deal with spiritual wickedness in high places in the name of Jesus Christ. Lord deal with those in places of authority that abuse their office they have either been chosen or went. Lord we ask that you restrain the wickedness of the enemy in the name of Jesus Christ and loose the bands of wickedness that the enemy desires to afflict upon those whom are working for you and allowing their lights to shine that others may see their light and be converted to Jesus Christ. Lord we ask you to deal with those accident scenes in which a physical clue is not left for the crime scene investigators to follow the lead. Lord we ask you to deal with those knowing the Word of God, yet confessing that you dwell within, and are knowingly practicing what is contrary to the Word of God in deed and in word. Lord we ask you to deal with those found in this area and deal with them accordingly in the name of Jesus. "Great is the Lord and Greatly to be praised; for your greatness is unsearchable." Lord we ask that our nests are filled with good things that are of you and pleasing in your sight in the name of Jesus Christ. Lord in the Old Testament many Kings brought down the high places that were built and we ask you in the name of Jesus Christ that the high places that the true enemy, the adversary and those confessing salvation whom allow the adversary to use them will be brought down in the name of Jesus. Lord thank you in the name of Jesus Christ for bringing these walls down in the name of Jesus Christ. Lord even walls that are not visible to me that the enemy is building in the name of Jesus Christ. Satan the Lord rebuke you in the name of Jesus Christ. Revelations 12:11 states, **"And they overcame him by the blood**

23

of the Lamb, and by the word of their testimony." Greater is He, Jesus, that is within me than he that is in the world because ye are of God, little children, and have overcome them (I John 4:4). I praise God for realizing whatever the situation; you Lord are greater than the situation. Lord we loose the special machinery to deal with these situations in the name of Jesus. Lord thank you for being the Shepherd and Bishop of our Souls. **Therefore Jesus Christ is the only Bishop, Shepherd and Bishop of our Souls that is sitting on the right hand of His Father, God. Let Jesus Christ whom dwells inside of you be your Bishop and Shepherd, Healer, Deliverer, Strong-tower, Redeemer, Provider, Provisionary, Stronghold, and my only Mediator.** Lord we ask you to deal with the spiritually wicked and releaser of imagination forces that would cause one to look at the same sex for relationships. Lord we cast down imaginations and everything that exalts itself above and against the knowledge of Jesus Christ in the name of Jesus Christ. Lord we ask you to suffocate the demonic forces and brain altering demons in the name of Jesus Christ. Lord we ask you to clean the house and then protect the house with your shield of faith from the entry of seven times more than it had in the name of Jesus Christ. Allow those freed and delivered from these forces to walk upright, close to you Lord, and most importantly in the fear of you Lord.

The word of the Lord states in **Proverbs 19:23, "The fear of the Lord tendeth to life: and he that hath it shall abide satisfied; he shall not be visited with evil.**

Lord allow us to fear you the more with trembling in the name of Jesus. Lord we thank you that because we fear you, Jesus abides in me, and Jesus word abides in me, I shall be satisfied and no evil shall visit me in the name of Jesus Christ. Lord we Praise and bless your Holy name because you deserve all the glory, honour, and power for thou hast created all things for thy pleasure they are were created in the name of Jesus. Allow the lights of those in authority to glow in you Lord in the name of Jesus Christ and those that refuse to line up with the Word of God, Lord we ask you to deal with them in the name of Jesus Christ. Lord we speak life in the name of Jesus Christ. **Proverbs 18:21 states, the Power of Life and death lies in the tongue** in the name of Jesus Christ. I believe and proclaim **Psalms 118:17, I shall not die, but live to declare the works of the Lord** in the name of Jesus Christ. Lord we ask you in the name of Jesus Christ to deal with known and unknown wickedness and spiritual wickedness in the name of Jesus. Lord abort it's operation and restrain the users of it in the name of Jesus Christ.

## Prayer to Bind the Spirit of Jealousy

Father God in the name of Jesus Christ
Lord we ask you to deal with the spirit of jealousy and with the heart of the individual(s) in the name of Jesus Christ. The Word of God states in the book of **Songs of Solomon 8:6 states, "Set a seal upon thine heart, as a seal upon thine arm: for love is strong as death; jealousy is cruel as the grave: the coals of fire, which hath a most vehement flame.** Lord we ask you deal with hearts down to the root or core in the name of Jesus Christ. **Matthew 10:28 states, "And fear not them which kill the body, but are not able to kill the soul: but rather fear him, which is able to destroy both soul and body in hell. Jeremiah 17:9 states, "The heart is deceitful above all things, and desperately wicked: who can know it."** Lord we thank you that you know it, the hearts of all and are able to protect us in seen, unseen, known, and unknown danger in the name of Jesus Christ. Lord we thank you for the Word of God that states in **Jeremiah 17:10, "I the Lord search the heart, I try the reins, even to give every man according to the fruit of his doing.** Lord deal with minds, thought patterns, and thinking of these individuals thinking that God somehow gave them life that they can take another life in spirit or physically. Lord allow drops of the blood of Jesus to run through their blood flow in their brain and allow other tissues neurologically to be rectified, and corrected to line up with the Word of God in the name of Jesus Christ. Lord we loose the spirit of Love to replace the delivered places of hatred forces in the name of Jesus Christ. Lord you left on record letting us know that you know the intent of the heart, premeditations, desires, and wills before carried out. Lord we ask for exposure of the devises of the wicked and spiritually wicked in the name of Jesus Christ. Not limited to allowing the wicked and evil desire to fall upon them in the name of Jesus Christ. Lord we ask you to wash the hearts, vessels, and every part with these findings and others unknown at this time in the name of Jesus Christ. Lord deal also if somehow this was brought on by a psychological issue not dealt with or one that is being treated with medications. Lord we ask you to make the proper adjustments knowing that man was made by God and God knows the levels body wise that each individual should have personally. Just as He knows the strands of hair on our heads. Lord we trust and depend, by faith believe what we pray and thank you for answering this prayer in the name of Jesus Christ. Lord we ask you to look on those transitioning from ministries, during the transition if the soul watcher stops watching, Lord we thank you for **Psalms 121:3b "he that keepeth thee will not slumber"** and **"God is our refuge and strength, a very present help in the time of trouble" noted in Psalms 46:1** in the name of Jesus Christ. Lord we ask you in the name of Jesus, according **to Jeremiah 17:14 "Heal me, O Lord, and I shall be healed; save me, and I shall be saved: for thou art my praise** in the name of Jesus Christ. Heal them Lord from these problems before judgment falls upon them in the name of Jesus. Those that continue to refuse to comply we ask Lord, whatever it takes to deal with the issues at hand, let it be done in the name of Jesus Christ. Lord we thank you for the Word of God that lets us know that you are sharper than any two edged sword cutting the body, the soul, spirit, even down to the marrow. Lord we ask you to circumcise the heart, mold it, and renew it in the name of Jesus.

## Prayer to Heal Those Who Prey on Their Own Children

Father God in the name of Jesus Christ

Lord deal with those that prey on their own children, victims of extended hospital care and stay. Lord deal with the mind set and correct the sickness in the mind and we cast down the imaginations in the name of Jesus Christ. Lord, we loose these bands of wickedness in the mind and all other forces set up that promotes this behavior in the name of Jesus Christ. Lord you cast out many demons out of children and people while in the flesh on this earth. Lord you said in the Word of God greater works shall we do. Lord heal in the name of Jesus and we release your holy stones on the demonic forces in the name of Jesus Christ to grind them to powder in the name of Jesus Christ.

## Prayer of Preservation

Father God in the name of Jesus Christ

Lord we thank you for the Word of God that states in *II Timothy 1:7,* "For the which cause I also suffer these things: nevertheless I am not ashamed: for I know whom I have believed, and am persuaded that he is able to keep that which I have committed unto him against that day." Therefore you will keep what we submit to you and we thank you Lord in the name of Jesus. Lord we ask you to keep our minds and thoughts intact, our hearts pure, hands clean, and continue to renew the right spirit in us in the name of Jesus Christ. Lord, **Psalms 140:4 "Keep me, O Lord, from the hands of the wicked; preserve me from the violent man; who have purposed to overthrow my goings. Psalms 64:1 states, "Hear my voice, O God, in my prayer: preserve my life from fear of the enemy." II Timothy 21:7, For God hath not given us the spirit of fear; but of power, and of love, and of a sound mind. Psalms 84:2 states, "Preserve my soul; for I am holy: O thou my God, save thy servant that trusteth in thee. Psalms 121:7-8 states, "The Lord shall preserve thee from all evil: he shall preserve thy soul. The Lord shall preserve thy going out and thy coming in from this time forth, and even for evermore."** Lord I pray in the name of Jesus that our holy armour, the Shield of Faith will quench every fiery dart of the wicked and the Sword of the Spirit will sever, cut, break, abort, and make the desire of the enemy unrealized in the name of Jesus Christ.

## Prayer for Vertigo and Disorders That Cause Dizziness Affecting the Ability to Walk and Praise You Lord

Father God in the name of Jesus Christ. Praise is comely. Lord you commanded us in the Word of God "To make a joyful noise unto the Lord all ye lands; come before His presence with singing; know ye that the Lord He is God. Lord you commanded us in the Word of God to "Praise ye the Lord. Praise God in His sanctuary, Praise Him in the Firmament of His Power. Praise Him for His mighty acts: praise Him according to His excellent greatness. Praise Him with the sound of the trumpet: praise him with the psaltery and harp. Praise Him with the timbrel and dance: Praise Him with the string instruments and organs. Praise Him with loud cymbals. Praise Him upon the high sounding cymbals. Let everything that hath breath praise the LORD. Praise ye the Lord!

Lord when we praise you a sweet smelling savor is continuously flowing knowing **"From the rising of the sun unto the going down of the same the LORD's name is to be praised" according to Psalms 113:3.** Lord we ask you to regulate these disorders with just a drop of Jesus Holy Healing Blood in the name of Jesus Christ. Lord we ask you to dry up ear inflammation in the name of Jesus Christ. Lord we ask you to heal the vestibular system at the root of the problem with balance, nausea, and vomiting. Lord we ask you to regulate the labyrinth system which send signals of sound and balance to the brain in the name of Jesus. (Mayo Clinic, 2014 retrieved online @ http://www.mayoclinic.org/diseases-conditions/vertigo/basics/symptoms/con-20028216). Lord we also ask you to regulate and heal any imbalances or malfunctions with the anterior and posterior pituitary gland in the name of Jesus Christ. Lord, send your precious blood through the cerebellum and brain stem in the name of Jesus Christ. Lord we pray many will be healed, testify of your healing power, serve and worship you in the name of Jesus Christ.

## Prayer for the Diabetic

Father God in the name of Jesus Christ. Lord we ask you to breath on the pancreas, beta, and alpha cells and all mal or non-functioning organs like when you breathed the breath of life in Adam in the name of Jesus Christ. Lord we ask you to regulate sugar levels in people that have been diabetics for years for a testimony to you Lord. We ask that through the power of God, diet, weight loss and exercise they will be healed of this disease that may have eventually affected every organ negatively. Lord we bind the ability of vein and artery malfunction leading to heart and kidney problems in the name of Jesus Christ. Lord allow the shield of faith which quenches every fiery dart of the enemy and the Sword of the Spirit which is sharper than any two edged sword to be used to aid in the progress. Lord we curse diabetes in the name of Jesus Christ. Lord we suffocate the demonic forces working behind the scenes and we ask you to dry up this disease out of those whom are serving you indeed in the name of Jesus Christ. Lord we thank you that the blood sugars will be within normal range and they will comply with the healthy nutritious diets. If sweets are eaten make sure they eat them immediately after their meal and not for a single serving in the name of Jesus Christ. Lord we curse diabetes out of the family line in the name of Jesus Christ. Therefore in the name of Jesus Christ, diabetes stops were it is without the ability to affect any more in the generational line in the name of Jesus Christ.

## God Performed the First Surgery; Let Him Operate on You

## Prayer for Heart Problems

Search your heart and make sure your serving the true and living God

**Deuteronomy 6:4-5, Hear, O Israel: the Lord our God is one Lord. And thou shalt love the Lord thy God with all thine heart, and with all thy soul, and with all thy might.**

If the devil tells you this is not true quote

**Luke 4:8, And Jesus answered and said unto him, Get thee behind me Satan: for it is written, Thou shalt love the Lord thy God, and him only shalt thou serve.**

If the devil returns, then quote this scripture

**Romans 5:8, But God commendeth his love toward us, in that, while we were yet sinners, Christ died for us.**

If he returns, then quote this scripture

**John 15:13, Greater love hath no man than this, that a man lay down his life for his friends.**
**Psalms 107:20, "And He sent His word, and healed them, and delivered them from their destructions."**

Jesus came to destroy the works of the devil as noted in **I John 3:8**, "He that committeth sin is of the devil; for the devil **sinneth** from the beginning. For this purpose the Son of God was manifested, that he might destroy the works of the devil."

**"Behold, I give unto you power to tread on serpents and scorpions, and over all the power of the enemy: and nothing by any means shall hurt you" Luke 10:19.** (http://youtu.be/6ZUrfULik1U)

Father God in the name of Jesus, I command my heart to beat according to the Word of God just as the wheels are in line and intact with the angels and the sun and moon are in line with the Word of God and are on schedule. I ask and believe God will make the Heart he made and blessed me with to beat orderly so that I will be able to praise Him better in Jesus Name.

Step I - The ability to quote these scriptures out loud and believe them.
**I Timothy 2:5, "For there is one God, and one mediator between God and men, the man Christ Jesus."**

Romans 10:9, "That if thou shalt confess with thy mouth the Lord Jesus, and shalt believe in thine heart that God hath raised him from the dead, thou shalt be saved."

Psalms 113:4, "The Lord is high above all nations, and his glory above the heavens. Who is like unto the Lord our God, who dwelleth on high?"

## II - You must want to be made well
John 5:6, "When Jesus saw him lie, and knew that he had been now a long time in that case, he saith unto him, Wilt thou be made whole?"

## III - Must believe God made man from the dust of the ground
Genesis 2:7, "And the Lord God formed man of the dust of the ground, and breathed into his nostrils the breath of life; and man became a living soul."

## IV - Must believe in the first surgery on man by God
Genesis 2:21, "And the Lord God caused a deep sleep to fall upon Adam and he slept: and he took one of his ribs, and closed up the flesh instead thereof; And the rib, which the Lord God had taken from man, made he a woman, and brought her unto the man."

## V - Hide the Word In Your Heart
Psalms 119:11, "Thy word have I hid in mine heart, that I might not sin against thee."

## VI - Make sure your fruit is healthy and edible
Galatians 5:22, "But the fruit of the Spirit is love, joy, peace, longsuffering, gentleness, goodness, faith, Meekness, temperance: against such there is no law."

## VII - Make sure your thinking on those things that are true, honest, just, pure, lovely, and of a good report
Philippians 4:8, "Finally, brethren, whatsoever things are true, whatsoever things are honest, whatsoever things are just, whatsoever things are pure, whatsoever things are lovely, whatsoever things are of good report; if there be any virtue, and if there be any praise, think on these things."

## VIII - When your mind begins to drift in areas it shouldn't bring it back into focus with the Word of God and rebuke the devil in the name of Jesus.
Isaiah 26:3, "Thou wilt keep him in perfect peace, whose mind is stayed on thee; because he trusteth in thee."

## Search my heart
Jeremiah 17:9, "The heart is deceitful above all things, and desperately wicked: who can know it?"
One drop of the pure, holy blood of Jesus Christ will cleanse these hearts and make them pure, moldable, and shapeable for the Lord.

RECEIVE *the* BLOOD *of* JESUS TRANSFUSION

MATTHEW 26:28

King James Bible: Authorized Version; Cambridge Edition

For this is my blood of the new testament, which is shed for many for the remission of sins:

NO APPOINTMENT NEEDED

But as many as received him, to them gave he power to become the sons of God, even to them that believe on his name: John 1:12

ONLY TAKES ONE DROP OF THE BLOOD OF JESUS TO PURIFY AND CLEANSE YOUR BLOOD

Neither by the blood of goats and calves, but by his own blood he entered in once into the holy place, having obtained eternal redemption for us HEBREWS 9:12

www.youtube.com/watch?v=rdOlt9K9ywY

Circumcise my heart and all needed areas to remove everything that is not pleasing to you God and "**create in me a clean heart, O God; and renew a right spirit within me**" according to Psalms 51:10.

## When You Want Your Heart to Die Prayer
Prayer for Suicidal Ideations

**John 10:10b** – "**I am come that they might have life, and that they might have it more abundantly.** Therefore, Jesus Christ died for me on the cross that I may live abundantly. Jesus is love and he loves me because I was made in the image of God's eyes. I am unique and there is no one anywhere in the world just like me. Every thing may not or is not perfect with me but the Word of God says he shall perfect those things, which concern me according to **Psalms 138:8. "The LORD will perfect that which concerneth me: thy mercy, O LORD, endureth for ever: forsake not the works of thine own hands." Numbers 23:19 "God is not a man, that he should lie; neither the son of man, that he should repent: hath he said, and shall he not do it? Or hath he spoken and shall he not make it good?** I believe that Jesus is the Son of the living God and he loves me more than I love myself. We go through things in life but it does not compare to the suffering Christ endured before, during and on the Cross. John 15:13 states, "Greater love hath no man than this, that a man lay down his life for his friends." I ask God to perfect those things concerning me, clean my heart, wash me clean with the blood of Jesus, and allow me to serve and worship Him, the true and living God. I ask God to get me back on track so I can effectively serve and worship him in spirit and truth. Job endured the trial and God restored him with more than he loss.

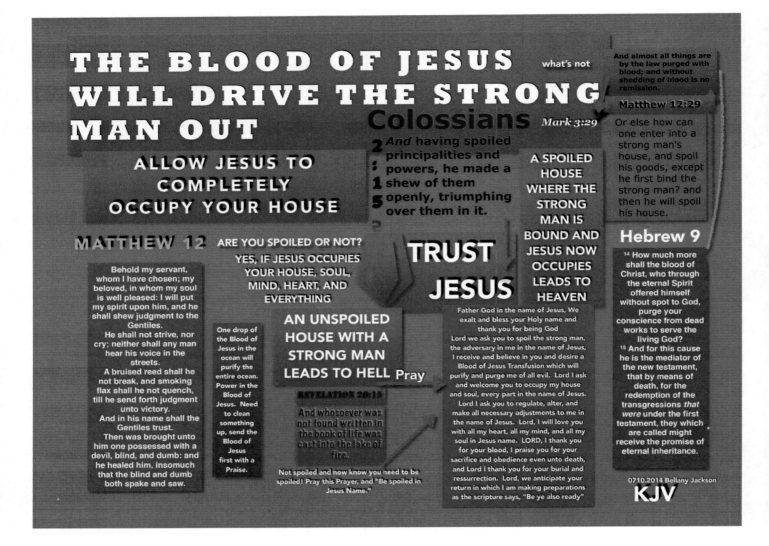

The surgeon Jesus is ready and available in the pre-op area to start your IV and for you to mark the site of the surgery but because God made you, He knows the other problems too, than just the one you think you have. Hopefully you will consent to Jesus doing what He wants on all your other parts too and you will be transformed as the scripture says, **"Create in me a clean heart and renew a right spirit in me."** The scripture says in **Romans 12:2, "be ye transformed by the renewing of your mind, that ye may prove what is that good, and acceptable and perfect will of God." Romans 12:9 says, "Let love be without dissimulation. Abhor that which is evil; cleave to that which is good." Cleave to God and those things which are good."** The bible says in **Psalms 100:5, "For the Lord is good; his mercy is everlasting; and his truth endureth to all generations."** We are to hate those things, which are evil. Should I hate my brother or should I hate his ways? We are to love everybody but not be bosom buddies with everyone. Yes, I can speak to you but will I invite you over for dinner? Most importantly, we should pray for them. What if you feel they are inflicting hardship or causing undesired burdens? If this be true, God is able to turn the situation around in your favor and undo the heavy burdens through fasting. Still be friendly and wait for God to move on your behalf. This too shall pass. When King David committed the sin of putting Bathsheba husband on the front line to cover up something. Nowhere in scripture did you read that Uriah family was trying get back at David for this. God knows how to handle the situation. Read the story. God knows where the deep, hard, soft, and fragile crevices and wholes are that no one knows exist in you. Just ask God to get them back and let you hear about, but don't rejoice when the downfall happens. King David got up and washed his face and ate, when it was all over and he, the King kept on living and serving God. We too must realize everything we go through is not because of wrong we have done. The Word of God states in Job that God asked Satan have you considered my servant Job? Read the story.

## Prayer for Those, People Are Trying to Mentally Kill

This prayer for those you can sit on an airplane with one person on each side and they both began to use some type of witchcraft on you, which you feel it in your body. This prayer for those who hear voices that seem to try to instruct them to do something they know is wrong. For example, you can be in a shoe store and have the money to pay for what you need and this evil, deceiving voice speaks and says just take them. This prayer is for those whom know what's right but the adversary the devil continues to pull at your brain and when the pressure exceeds your good will, a negative result may occur. The bible says the devil came not but for to steal, to kill, and to destroy. His desire is to hurt you physically, mentally, shame you and your family. The Lord rebuke the enemy in the name of Jesus Christ. Just remember God gave you life, Jesus is Life, and we live through Him. We as Christians are to endure hardness as a good soldier. Can you find a weary soldier on the battlefield? Weary in mental and physical strength and stamina. The bible states "Be not weary in well doing, you shall reap if you faint not. The bible states, "There is one God, one mediator between God and men, the man Christ Jesus. If somehow you're not walking with the true and living God and serving the man, Jesus, that suffered, hung, bled, and died for you, it's now time to get right (Jesus Holy, Heavy Steps, http://www.cdbaby.com/cd/bellanyjackson1). God can reach you where you are and give you peace and forgiveness. Be found doing good and allow Jesus the light and Life to reign in your lives. Psalms 119:105, Thy word is a lamp unto my feet, and a light unto my path.

When your defenses, for example in you body are down, if you come in contact with the flu, your chances of catching it increases. When you are mentally drained or challenged, if you don't know God and are not trusting in Him, unwarranted things may happen. When you are going through a mentally challenging time in your life, pick up the bible and read it. Quote **Isaiah 26:3, "Thou wilt keep him in perfect peace, whose mind is stayed on thee: because he trusteth in thee."** The problem is the enemy was mentally challenging you and the remedy is perfect peace. How can you receive this peace? **John 14:27, "Peace I leave with you, my peace I give unto you: not as the world giveth, give I unto you. Let not your heart be troubled, neither let it be afraid. God wants to give you this peace.** The Word of God states **in John 3:16, "For God so loved the world that He gave His only begotton Son, that whosoever believeth in Him should not perish, but have everlasting life."** God gave His only begotton Son, Jesus to suffer mentally, physically, psychologically, and every other way, so you and I could receive this peace. You must receive Christ first in order to receive this peace. The Word of God states, **This is the stone which was set at nought of you builders, which is become the head of the corner. Neither is there salvation in any other: for there is none other name under heaven given among men, whereby we must be saved (Acts 4:11-12). "For it is written, As I live, saith the Lord, every knee shall bow to me, and every tongue shall confess to God" noted in Romans 14:11.** Regardless of how you used your tongue or what you spoke, your mouth shall speak that Jesus Christ is Lord and the best part, you will be able to see Him then. The Word of God states, every eye shall see no matter what part of the earth you're in, all will see Jesus.

Get right with Jesus and He will fix your mind.

## "Let Us Celebrate Dr. Martin Luther King, Jr. The King That Served The King of Kings"

**Praise the Lord**

# REV. DR. MARTIN LUTHER KING, JR.
## "DR. KING WHO SERVED THE KING OF KINGS"

**JESUS**

### Ephesians

10 Finally, my brethren, be strong in the Lord, and in the power of his might.
11 Put on the whole armour of God, that ye may be able to stand against the wiles of the devil.
12 For we wrestle not against flesh and blood, but against principalities, against powers, against the rulers of the darkness of this world, against spiritual wickedness in high *places*.
13 Wherefore take unto you the whole armour of God, that ye may be able to withstand in the evil day, and having done all, to stand.
14 Stand therefore, having your loins girt about with truth, and having on the breastplate of righteousness;

*- King James Bible "Authorized Version", Cambridge Edition*

LET US CELEBRATE MARTIN LUTHER KING, JR.

THE KING WHO LOVED THE KING OF KINGS

LET US CELEBRATE MARTIN LUTHER KING, JR.

DR. KING WHO WORE THE ARMOUR/SPIRITUAL WEAPONS

OF THE KING OF KINGS AND THE LORD DELIVERED

**Ephesians 6:10-20**

LET US CELEBRATE MARTIN LUTHER KING, JR.

A VESSEL WHO MINISTERED AND SPOKE THE WORD OF GOD

LET US CELEBRATE MARTIN LUTHER KING, JR., LIFE IN THE FLESH

WHO SERVED THE WORD MADE FLESH AND DWELT AMONG US, JESUS CHRIST

WHO CUTS IRON, BREAKS BRASS, AND DESTROYS EVERY YOKE

LET US CELEBRATE DR. MARTIN LUTHER KING, JR.

WHOSE LEAD BY EXAMPLE OF NONVIOLENCE BROUGHT ABOUT CHANGE

LET US CELEBRATE DR. MARTIN LUTHER KING, JR.

WHO MARRIED CORRETTA SCOTT KING AND WAS FRUITFUL AND MULTIPLIED THE LAND

LET US CELEBRATE DR. MARTIN LUTHER KING, JR.

HONORARY DEGREES, NOBEL PEACE PRIZE, AND DEGREES IN WHICH WE GIVE THE LORD PRAISE

LET US CELEBRATE DR. MARTIN LUTHER KING, JR.

FOR GOD WAS WITH HIM FROM THE PROTESTS, PRISON, ATTEMPTS, AND ALL THE WAY TO THE STATE CAPITAL

AND EVEN NOW TO BE ABSENT FROM THE BODY IS TO BE PRESENT WITH THE LORD

LET US CELEBRATE GOD AND JESUS CHRIST, THE KING OF KINGS, FOR SENDING AND USING REV. DR. MARTIN LUTHER KING, JR.

### 6:10-20

15 And your feet shod with the preparation of the gospel of peace;
16 Above all, taking the shield of faith, wherewith ye shall be able to quench all the fiery darts of the wicked.
17 And take the helmet of salvation, and the sword of the Spirit, which is the word of God:
18 Praying always with all prayer and supplication in the Spirit, and watching thereunto with all perseverance and supplication for all saints;
19 And for me, that utterance may be given unto me, that I may open my mouth boldly, to make known the mystery of the gospel,
20 For which I am an ambassador in bonds: that therein I may speak boldly, as I ought to speak.

*- King James Bible "Authorized Version", Cambridge Edition*

**HJN** Pastor Bellany Jackson

Bellany Jackson Copyright 2015 **BJP**

# ANIMAL CRUELTY PREVENTION & AWARENESS PRAYER

Praise the Lord

JESUS

FATHER GOD IN THE NAME OF JESUS CHRIST. LORD WE THANK YOU FOR EVERY LIVING THING YOU MADE IN WHICH ALL WAS MADE BEFORE MAN. THE WORD OF GOD STATES GENESIS 1:28, "AND GOD BLESSED THEM, AND GOD SAID UNTO THEM, BE FRUITFUL, AND MULTIPLY, AND REPLENISH THE EARTH, AND SUBDUE IT: AND HAVE DOMINION OVER THE FISH OF THE SEA, AND OVER THE FOWL OF THE AIR, AND OVER EVERY LIVING THING THAT MOVETH UPON THE EARTH." LORD WHEN THE WORLD WAS DESTROYED BY WATER, NOAH WAS INSTRUCTED BY YOU TO SAVE TWO OF EACH ANIMAL (MALE AND FEMALE) WHICH INSURED REPRODUCTION AS WITH NOAH'S FAMILY ON THE ARK WITH HIS WIFE AND THREE SONS AND THEIR WIVES INSURED REPRODUCTION FOR MANKIND. LORD ALLOW US TO SHOW LOVE TO

THE CHILDREN, DOGS, CATS, AND ALL ANIMALS. LET CHILD OR ANIMAL ABUSE/NEGLECT NOT BE FOUND IN THE HOUSE HOLD OF FAITH AND WORLDWIDE IN THE NAME OF JESUS CHRIST IN WHICH THESE COMPANIES CARE FOR ALL. MOST OF ALL LORD IT HAS BEEN STATED THERE IS A CORRELATION BETWEEN ANIMAL ABUSE AND CHILD ABUSE/NEGLECT. LORD DEAL WITH THE MINDS FIRST OF THOSE FOUND IN THIS SITUATION AND GIVE THEM AN OPPORTUNITY TO MAKE THE PROPER CORRECTIONS. DURING THIS STAGE ALSO ALLOW THEM TO HEAR A SPOKEN WORD CONCERNING THE MATTER IN WHICH THEY WILL KNOW IT WAS FOR THEM. IF THEY THEN REFUSE TO CHANGE WE ASK FOR EXPOSURE IN JESUS NAME. WE ASK THAT LOVING PEOPLE WILL INCREASE THE ADOPTION PERCENTAGE BY 50% IN 2015 WHICH WILL DECREASE THE EUTHANIZATION RATE OF ANIMALS AND WE ASK FOR A 100% REDUCTION IN CHILD ABUSE IN THE NAME OF JESUS CHRIST. WE ALSO ASK FOR A DECREASE IN SPAYING AND NEUTERING WITH THE ADOPTION RATE INCREASE IN GREAT HOMES SO THEY WON'T BE DEPRIVED OF REPRODUCING. LORD, IF NEGLECTED OR ABUSED CHILDREN ARE INVOLVED I ASK FOR THEIR RESCUE SOONER TO ENSURE PROPER CARE, STABILITY, AND NUTRITION. LORD ALLOW THIS ANIMAL CRUELTY PREVENTION AND AWARENESS PROGRAM TO EDUCATE, PREVENT AND IDENTIFY ABUSE/NEGLECT EARLY, WITH AN INCREASE IN EARLY REPORTING AND IDENTIFICATION LEADING TO RESCUE WITH THE ABILITY TO HEAL THE WOUNDS "FOR YOU ARE THE LORD THY GOD WHICH HEALETH THEE." ALSO KNOWING WHEN TO TURN YOUR ANIMAL IN DUE TO BITES, AND OTHER UNFORESEEN OCCURRENCES WHICH COULD LEAD TO MALNUTRITION NOT INTENTIONALLY, UNLESS YOU HAD OTHER ARRANGEMENTS IN PLACE FOR CARE DURING YOUR CRISIS. LORD ANYTHING WE FAILED TO MENTION IN THE PRAYER WE ASK YOU TO DEAL WITH THOSE AREAS TOO.

LORD WE THANK YOU FOR ALL THINGS AND FOR THE EARLY PREVENTION AND AWARENESS OF ANIMAL AND CHILD ABUSE IN JESUS MIGHTY, HOLY NAME WE PRAY. AMEN.

HJN
Pastor Bellany Jackson

BJP
Copyright 2015

How to approach this section remember the scripture **Matthew 12:33, "Either make the tree good, and his fruit good; or else make the tree corrupt, and his fruit corrupt: for the tree is known by his fruit."**

If you are known or have been labeled corrupt, allow Jesus to make you good by getting on the strait gate or narrow road which leads to life times two. If you are good with good fruit, continue, stay in the Word of God and stay prayed up, lest you may fall! If you the tree is good indeed and enemies have labeled you corrupt, God will deal with this by refining good fruit the more as evidenced allowing you to shine and not be placed **"under a bushel, but on a candlestick; and it giveth light unto all that are in the house."**

*Matthew 5:15-16*
[15] **Neither do men light a candle, and put it under a bushel, but on a candlestick; and it giveth light unto all that are in the house.** [16] **Let your light so shine before men, that they may see your good works, and glorify your Father which is in heaven.**

**Application** – Make the tree good! Make the tree good! Make the tree good! You are the tree. Let Jesus be your foundation, the firm solid unshakeable, undefeatable solid rock whom is the Image of the Invisible God. Remember God made you and knows all about you, nothing is hidden, unspoken thoughts, desires, aspirations are all known to God. Receive your healing by allowing Jesus Christ and the power in the blood of Jesus Christ to cleanse and save you from your destructions and destroy yokes designed to cause you to get off track in the name Jesus Christ.

**What is a yoke?**
In the natural sense one would think of an egg yoke, which provides nutrients to our body. "Eggs are also high in sulfur, an essential nutrient that helps with everything from vitamin B absorption to liver function. But sulfur is also necessary for the production of collagen and keratin, which help create and maintain shiny hair, strong nails and glowing skin." (Retrieved 0805. 2014 http://www.huffingtonpost. com/2013/03/30/health-benefits-of-eggs-yolks_n_2966554.html)

A yoke is anything the adversary the devil can place within you to cause you harm or place in an individual(s) close to you to harm you for them. This wicked yoke goal is to destroy you, cause problems for you, not limited to loss of life. This yoke may be placed from someone in the world that does not know God or could be by a spiritual leader through spiritual wickedness in high places, wickedness in the workforce, or a hater without cause. Some yokes if you're not consistent in Christ you may not know they have been launched, meaning subtle, but once realized you must act immediately to recover successfully. Stay consistent in Jesus Christ and the Word the God. JESUS said my yoke is easy and my burden is light. **Isaiah 58:6** said, **"Is not this the fast I have chosen? to loose the bands of wickedness, to undo heavy burdens, and to let the oppressed go free, and to break every yoke.** This is accomplished by believing, receiving, fasting, praying, and trusting in Jesus Christ. Receive, Jesus, the only wicked yoke breaker and receive the easy yoke from Jesus Christ. You have to give up something. You are giving up the wicked ways of the world, which would have led you to hell, receiving Jesus ensuring your name is written in the Lamb's Book of Life. The old man must be bound and cast out to allow Jesus to occupy the space as evidenced by **Mark 3:27 which states, "No man can enter into a strong man's house, and spoil his goods, except he will first bind the strong man; and then he will spoil his house."** They both cannot stay in one soul. You must choose whom you will serve. Jesus Christ is life and leads to life times two, leads to heaven, leads to eternal life. Please note there was wickedness in the heart of the earth and God sent pure Jesus Christ to purify the place, three days and three nights and then raised Him first, then those being unjustly held, and gave Satan boundaries of where he could reside, until his lake of fire experience which is soon to come.

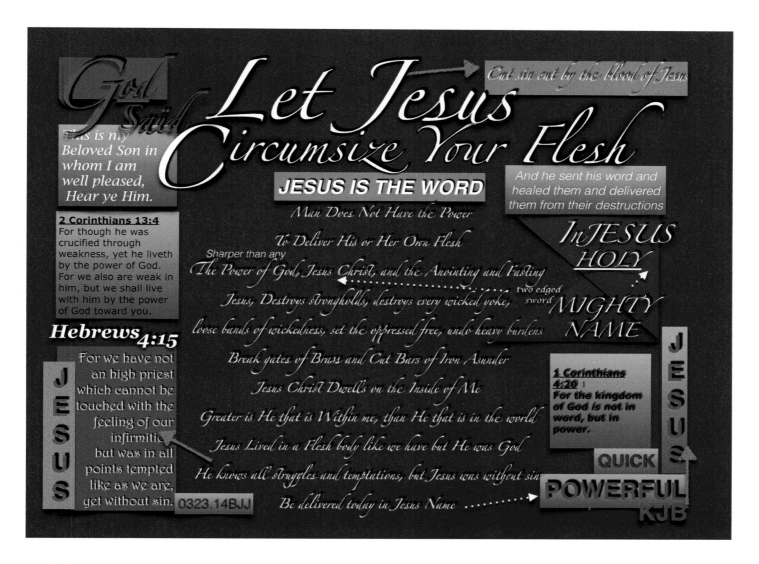

Before Jesus Christ was sent by God into the heart of the earth it was occupied by Satan and his demons holding captive some things, which belonged to God. That Holy pure vessel Jesus, the light shined in the darkness, the band loosener loosed the bands of wickedness, and purified the heart of the earth, God raised Jesus then those held captive were released, and satan was given boundaries of where he could reside, "**Prince of the power of the air, the spirit that now worketh in the children of disobedience (Ephesians 2:2).**" Satan is already defeated and "**And the devil that deceived them was cast into the lake of fire and brimstone, where the beast and the false prophet are, and shall be tormented day and night for ever and ever**" noted in Revelation 20:10.

God already stated, "**I have created the waster to destroy (Isaiah 54:16).**" In the next verse **Isaiah 54:17, "No weapon formed against me shall prosper; and every tongue that shall rise against thee in judgment thou shalt condemn. This is the heritage of the servants of the LORD, and their righteousness is of me**," saith the Lord." The Holy Savior of the World, Jesus purified the heart of the earth and Heaven was already purified when as noted in **Luke 10:18, "And he said unto them, I beheld Satan as lightning fall from heaven.**" Our feet walk on the earth and **I Corinthians 3:11 states "For other foundation can no man lay than that is laid, which is Jesus Christ.**" The foundation Jesus Christ, raised from the heart of the earth, then later received up in glory, and currently sitting on the right hand of His Father, God.

# INCONQUERABLE JESUS

## Colossians 1:

15 Who is the image of the invisible God, the firstborn of every creature:
16 For by him were all things created, that are in heaven, and that are in earth, visible and invisible, whether *they be* thrones, or dominions, or principalities, or powers: all things were created by him, and for him:
17 And he is before all things, and by him all things consist.
18 And he is the head of the body, the church: who is the beginning, the firstborn from the dead; that in all *things* he might have the preeminence.
19 For it pleased *the Father* that in him should all fulness dwell;

BJP

## "Only Begotton Son of God"

### ROMANS 8:37

Nay, in all these things we are more than conquerors through him that loved us.

*King James Bible "Authorized Version", Cambridge Edition*

## Revelation 20:10

And the devil that deceived them was cast into the lake of fire and brimstone, where the beast and the false prophet *are*, and shall be tormented day and night for ever and ever.

HJN

One may consider a yoke as an attachment of an evil force to a believer in Jesus Christ whom without knowledge may lead them back into the world. When a man and woman, both believers' in Jesus Christ marry, one could say they are yoked together. When identical twins are conceived they are yoked together then split in utero. Some babies are born yoked with one body and two heads in which most cases if medically able are separated. When the black race was in slavery, this was considered a yoke of bondage. When one chooses to stay in sin, willful sin, you are attached to a yoke of sin which will lead to spiritual death, death, and an unquenchable fire in the end with the adversary the devil, if you don't turn back to God in time.

A yoke is suppression, depression, heavy burdens, bands of wickedness with iron, brass, and any other metals used by the enemy, but Jesus is the brass breaker, iron cutter, and yoke destroyer. One drop of the blood of Jesus, one slash from the sharper than any two edged sword, Jesus Christ, and turning your plate by fasting because some things come only by fasting and praying.

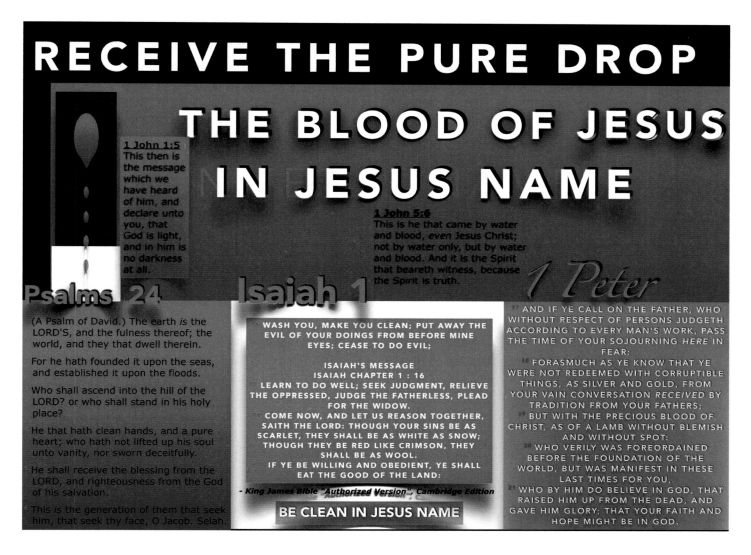

# RECEIVE THE PURE DROP

## THE BLOOD OF JESUS IN JESUS NAME

**1 John 1:5**
This then is the message which we have heard of him, and declare unto you, that God is light, and in him is no darkness at all.

**1 John 5:6**
This is he that came by water and blood, *even* Jesus Christ; not by water only, but by water and blood. And it is the Spirit that beareth witness, because the Spirit is truth.

### Psalms 24

(A Psalm of David.) The earth *is* the LORD'S, and the fulness thereof; the world, and they that dwell therein.

For he hath founded it upon the seas, and established it upon the floods.

Who shall ascend into the hill of the LORD? or who shall stand in his holy place?

He that hath clean hands, and a pure heart; who hath not lifted up his soul unto vanity, nor sworn deceitfully.

He shall receive the blessing from the LORD, and righteousness from the God of his salvation.

This *is* the generation of them that seek him, that seek thy face, O Jacob. Selah.

### Isaiah 1

WASH YOU, MAKE YOU CLEAN; PUT AWAY THE EVIL OF YOUR DOINGS FROM BEFORE MINE EYES; CEASE TO DO EVIL;

ISAIAH'S MESSAGE
ISAIAH CHAPTER 1 : 16
LEARN TO DO WELL; SEEK JUDGMENT, RELIEVE THE OPPRESSED, JUDGE THE FATHERLESS, PLEAD FOR THE WIDOW.
COME NOW, AND LET US REASON TOGETHER, SAITH THE LORD: THOUGH YOUR SINS BE AS SCARLET, THEY SHALL BE AS WHITE AS SNOW; THOUGH THEY BE RED LIKE CRIMSON, THEY SHALL BE AS WOOL.
IF YE BE WILLING AND OBEDIENT, YE SHALL EAT THE GOOD OF THE LAND:

*- King James Bible "Authorized Version", Cambridge Edition*

**BE CLEAN IN JESUS NAME**

### 1 Peter

[17] AND IF YE CALL ON THE FATHER, WHO WITHOUT RESPECT OF PERSONS JUDGETH ACCORDING TO EVERY MAN'S WORK, PASS THE TIME OF YOUR SOJOURNING *HERE* IN FEAR:
[18] FORASMUCH AS YE KNOW THAT YE WERE NOT REDEEMED WITH CORRUPTIBLE THINGS, AS SILVER AND GOLD, FROM YOUR VAIN CONVERSATION *RECEIVED* BY TRADITION FROM YOUR FATHERS;
[19] BUT WITH THE PRECIOUS BLOOD OF CHRIST, AS OF A LAMB WITHOUT BLEMISH AND WITHOUT SPOT:
[20] WHO VERILY WAS FOREORDAINED BEFORE THE FOUNDATION OF THE WORLD, BUT WAS MANIFEST IN THESE LAST TIMES FOR YOU,
[21] WHO BY HIM DO BELIEVE IN GOD, THAT RAISED HIM UP FROM THE DEAD, AND GAVE HIM GLORY; THAT YOUR FAITH AND HOPE MIGHT BE IN GOD.

What's connected to you! Is it for you or against you? At the end of the day are the goals met to ensure safety and well being to all? The God I serve allows one to repent and disconnect from the yoke or the Lord can separate, sever, abort, and make the yoke no longer existent. One must want to be delivered. The longer you stay attacked to a wicked yoke the further out in sin and further out of the will of God it may take you.

## Can't Hear From God Yoke

This yoke occurs when you are a spiritual leader or in ministry and you used to hear from God and now you are living a life of sin and cannot hear from God. Something is talking to you and you think it is God but the adversary has sent a force to make you think its God. In the scripture, God sent a prophet to King David regarding the sin concerning Bathsheba. King David could not hear from God and even as the prophet spoke to King David, He was still blind of His sin. The King was quick to respond on how the man should be punished for the sin. These sins still occur in churches today and you continue going to church listening to your Pastor and somehow don't know, they don't like you, they hate you, they want what you have, you are living holy and they are not, or some evil force has placed something in their mind and they have entertained it. If you stay too long knowing this you will surely die, freak accidents and they will preach your funeral and say wonderful things about you knowing in their heart they never liked you and wish you died sooner than now. Uriah is dead. Maybe the evil that was done to you in the House of God has already occurred, what can you do about it now. We are to make a sweet smelling savior in the nostrils of the Lord. The majority of these things were done in secret and now you pray for God to punish them in the open and let you know about it when it happens. When God punishes you for these sins, He will touch an area if I took matters in my own hands I would not reach. As you see, King David prayed and fasted for God's mercy concerning the child but it was not granted. I believe if He had restored the child this could have happened again. Some ask a question can God cause sickness to come upon you? The answer is Yes! II Samuel 12:15 And Nathan departed unto his house. And the LORD struck the child that Uriah's wife bare unto David, and it was very sick. Uriah was loyal to King David as noted in **II Samuel 11:11-12**

**¹¹ And Uriah said unto David, The ark, and Israel, and Judah, abide in tents; and my lord Joab, and the servants of my lord, are encamped in the open fields; shall I then go into mine house, to eat and to drink, and to lie with my wife? as thou livest, and as thy soul liveth, I will not do this thing.**

**¹² And David said to Uriah, Tarry here to day also, and to morrow I will let thee depart. So Uriah abode in Jerusalem that day, and the morrow.**

As you see, God dealt with the matter, a man could not have affected him as the Almighty God. A man would have felt like he had done something so great and had made such an impact when you didn't even touch the surface. This never happened again in King David's life when God was finished. Learn to give things to God no matter how sometimes you want so badly to injure, backstab, take vengeance in your own hands, God knows the truth of the matter regardless of what mouths say, even yours.

## Sickness Yoke

This yoke may be placed without your knowledge by family who is ready for you to die, someone who hates you within the body of Christ or in the world who does not know God. This yoke may be placed by someone you break bread with, sleep with, and could be the closest person to you. Also by one void of the understanding of scriptures practicing something called a transfer in which I rebuke in the Mighty Holy name of Jesus Christ. More explanation, when Jesus healed the ten lepers, they were healed without others having to be sick. Jesus healed fever, dried up bleeding, loosened death, opened blinded eyes, rebuked demons and commanded them to come out and released men, women, and children. Jesus healed not requiring another to be sick with whatever they were just delivered from and I rebuke the practice of anything contrary to the Word of God in the name of Jesus Christ. The Word of God states **3 John 1:2, "Beloved I wish above all things that thou mayest prosper and be in health even as thou soul prospereth.** The Word of God commands in **Psalms 150:6, "Let everything that hath breath, Praise ye the Lord! Psalms 33:1 states, "Rejoice in the LORD, O ye righteous: *for* praise is comely for the upright.**

## Homosexual Yoke

This yoke so sad to say is sometimes launched within the body of Christ through Spiritual Wickedness in High places and if your foot is not planted by the rivers of water that the Word of God states in Psalms you may be uprooted. Some of these leaders have launched these forces on so many people that now God is allowing it to affect their own family.

The yoke is also sent out through the World system that has an agenda to infect as many as possible with incurable diseases and to go against the Word of God in the book of Genesis. God placed one Adam and one Eve in the Garden of Eden noted in the book of Genesis.

The yoke may be placed in a funeral setting. You are paying respects to the family and part of the family may have an evil intent for you and your family. These yokes can be launched in this setting, you hug the grieving family with good, Godly intents and they are trying to hurt you and you don't even know it. But in do time or season the Lord reveals details of the releaser and the intent. You must pray, petition God, rebuke the enemy and declare that the protection of the Lord on you and your family in the name of Jesus. Just as Jesus through the power of God dried up the woman's issue of blood (**Luke 8:43-48**), which she received through her faith, he is able to dry up, grind to powder, drop a Holy stone on it and then you can praise the Lord in the dust. Giving glory to God and Jesus Christ for being head of all principalities and powers, a prayer answering and delivering God. You need to pull out your bible and allow your eyes to read the Word of God. This will clean your eyes and also ask God to cover or saturate your eyes with the blood of Jesus. Your mind is next, He whose mind is stayed on Him, He will keep in perfect peace. Are you fantasizing about ungodly things? You must cast down the imaginations. Be strong in the Lord and the power of Him might. You must first let God know you are nothing without Him and that you need Him. This is nothing one can conquer alone, one may try, but when Jesus heals the situation it is healed indeed, in which I am more than a conqueror through Christ Jesus my Lord.

The Word of God states in **II Corinthians 10:5, Casting down imaginations and everything that exalteth itself against the knowledge of God, and bringing into captivity every thought to the obedience of Christ. James 4:7** states you must, **"Submit yourself to God. Resist the devil, and he will flee from you."** Resist the devil now by the power of Jesus Christ and Live. Satan's end and his followers end is the Lake of Fire. Be Found in the Book of Life.

## Political Yokes of Homosexually

These yokes are placed because the world feels like they have to turn you away from the truth in the Word of God that they know dwells within you. They feel if they can change you they can get the laws that are contrary to the Word of God passed with the Holy Bible sitting in the courtroom. The bible that if asked by these noble men and woman could quote scripture and take you to the place in bible that confirms that it goes against the plan of God.

Also the bible speaks of the destruction of Sodom and Gomorrah. It will happen again, meaning things that were done there may be going on today and God has promised not to the destroy the World with water again. It doesn't matter the number of hurricane's that comes or floods. The world will never be destroyed by water, total destruction. The world will be destroyed by fire and if those who know God that sits in places of politics are fearful to speak about the truth. The truth is one day everyone will have to give an account to God for every idle word and deed. Regardless of whether you are the only one who knows about it, God knows. The Lord is head of all principalities and powers, head of all powers in heaven and in earth, and head of man, and the True and Living God, our Creator is pleased the fulness dwells in Jesus Christ. Judgment day is coming just like the travail of a woman with child not knowing when the water will break or where. She hopes it will break at the hospital where she can be refreshened and medical attention is available. Where will you be when judgment day comes? Choose this day whom you will serve! God or Mammon. The Word of God states that men will become lover's of themselves (II Timothy 3:1-5). **Matthew 5:18 states, "For verily I say unto you, Till heaven and earth pass, one jot or one tittle shall in no wise pass from the law, till all be fulfilled."**

It still is an abomination in the eye sight of God and any believers and receivers of Jesus Christ should see it the same but realizing these people still have a soul to be delivered, converted, and saved (Receive Salvation through Jesus Christ).

## Political Yokes

This yoke is one elected or placed in a position in the government to fulfill a duty. Their duty is clear and they may have taken an oath to do right by the people. Then discord may have come because there are other parties not in the government with agenda's and they have attached themselves to the people in office. Anytime one is attached to a wicked yoke with an agenda to derail, disrespect, and somehow in their thinking, that they would suppress one whose Oath is greater than all whom is the Office of the United States. The duties must be fulfilled. Therefore if a way or provision was made to bypass some that need to be delivered from this yoke, Praise the Lord! The Word of God states, "why sit we here until we die." There was famine if they went back into one camp and there was war if they went the other way. Or they could sit there and do nothing and die. Thank God the men went into the camp and the fighting was over and they were able to pick up spoils of the war, which are precious metals and other valuables. Some could not fathom what goes on in a day of some of the highest Officials and yet in the midst of all of this, others are still on there post watching out for the safety of the US while you sleep, reap havoc, speak negative, and stir discord. Remember this, the Lord still opens holes in the earth without warning to those whom it is designed for.

Ask the Lord to detach you from the yokes that are contrary and ask Him to bring back the unity and respect that once was there before His judgment falls in Jesus name.

## Mental Yoke

**Put** on your **Helmet of Salvation** and Keep your mind stayed on Him (scriptures, psalms of praise, songs of praise! **Put on** your **Shield of Faith** that **quenches every fiery dart of the enemy**!

This yoke is designed to flood your mind with problems or experiences you have just gone through and some of which you have been delivered but the enemy desire is for them to consume your mind again. You have gone to God and asked him to remove things from your mind, thinking maybe you have forgiven the one who caused them. Every time you began a constructive task the enemy the devil keeps bringing the same thoughts back to your mind and it seems to remain. The goal of the enemy is to paralysis you and your thinking on just the negative but Jesus states I came that you might have Life and have it more abundantly. This is when you began to quote the scriptures each time it comes to mind and tell God, You said in the Word of God that the anointing breaks the yokes and this includes other yokes I don't even know are there. **Isaiah 54:6** states, "**Is not this the fast I have chosen? to loose the bands of wickedness, to let the oppressed go free, to undo heavy burdens, and to BREAK EVERY YOKE.**" Your helmet is for safety and protection while driving, working, especially during spiritual warfare from attacks from the enemy but the power of God will hold you up in the name of Jesus Christ.

## Loosing a Love One Yoke With Shame

The family with a loss of a loved one to a brutal death, an infamous infection or from living a lifestyle that in contrary to the Word of God. Some feel that certain things cannot happen to them but yet rejoiced when you went through some hardships. The bible states in **Proverbs 24:17** "**Rejoice not when thine enemy falleth, and let not thine heart be glad when he stumbleth.**" Did you get pleasure out of someone's child going to jail, hearing in mist of a robbery the individual was shot and killed, did you rejoice to see someone lose there home, did you rejoice when you aided in the death of someone because you wanted the insurance money or just didn't want to be bothered anymore, did you prey on an innocent soul that came to your church seeking salvation, seeking a closer relationship to Christ and you aided or allowed members knowingly direct them away from the still waters and paths of righteousness. Yet spiritual leaders think they somehow are exempt from punishment from God for their wrong. King David, the only King in scripture God states "a man after God's own heart," stated He hid the Word of God in his heart that He would not sin against it. A prophet came to him ordered by God (**II Samuel** 11-12) to address a situation, and at another time David was given three choices for punishment for another sin. In which he chose punishment from God (**I Chronicles** 21:1-30) because he stated God was merciful.

## Lust Yokes

Sad to say, this yoke is released in the house of God through spiritual wickedness in high places and from the world, even teachers. You could be working or sitting in church and suddenly you would have a lust attack and seems so real. This could be released in the workforce or anyplace. It is designed to break your concentration. This force is also launched in schools to distract some from receiving the education their parents secured or others have chosen. This force could be released from a jealous Bishop trying to derail another pastor that he knows is Bishop status. This yoke makes you want a certain individual or either makes you want to engage in practices that the Word of God speaks against. It is a demonic spirit sent by an individual. One may ask God to destroy the forces working through the individuals not limited to the individual whom is allowing Satan to use them whom knew better or ask for them to be delivered. If not dealt with may lead to your demise.

There is a holy stone that the Word of God speaks of and the Word of God states that it will grind those forces to powder. You need to ask God to drop a holy stone on the forces. It is important when you pray that there is nothing we are doing to block our prayers from being heard. Satan hates anyone that loves God. You could have a best friend, spiritual leader, hater, that is envious of your relationship with God and they want to be close to you so they can find the avenue to halt your walk with God. Remember, the Word of God states in **Proverbs 15:3 "The eyes of the Lord are in every place, beholding the evil and the good."** Our desire should be to please God, worship and praise God and Jesus during and especially at the end of this earthly life and that our names are written in the Lamb's Book of Life which secures placement in Heaven.

## Educational Yokes

This yoke is evil, as are the others. This yoke is designed to start you in a field of study without completing it. It's almost like running a marathon and you are 2-3 feet from the finish line and just those few steps cannot be made to finish. This yoke is launched out by some in the House of God, could be leaders, principals, district office, other people in the education field that just don't like the God in you, or either through the educational realm. There desire is to suppress you and try to hold you hostage and keep their foot on you because of the God in you, if you are a believer in God. But remember, when God returns to them there evil, don't rejoice, but just know He is still on the throne ruling. NO ONE IS ABOVE GOD. No one in the world is above God. As you talk to people in high places of stature or position, one may feel belittled or less because of the title. But just remember, they will have to stand before the same God you will stand before and give an account in the Judgment. You may have a bosom buddy that you tell all your goals, dreams, and desires and you don't know, but someone has tried to tell you that they hate you. You continue with this friend, relationship, and the final goal of the enemy is mental suicide. Before you were so focused and now, you almost wrecked, just can't get out of bed, or better yet during your study you are becoming more distracted. The enemy came to steal, kill, and destroy but **Jeremiah 29:11 states "I know the thoughts that I think toward you, saith the Lord, thoughts of peace, and not of evil, and to give you an expected end."** The expected and desired final end for every Child of God should be eternal life with God in heaven while living on this earth with obedience to God, joy, having all needs and desires met by our Heavenly Father by Christ Jesus Our Lord and Savior with prosperity.

## Test Taking Yokes

This yoke is sometimes placed through spiritual leaders or through the church, by haters, through the school program your attending, or professor wickedness or your closest friends and relatives that you have befriended with only good intentions and their desire is to get inside your mind to prevent you from passing your exam. These demons are released to cause a focus malfunction and distract you during testing. They are released sometimes through the ventilator system via the air in which Satan is the Prince of the Air. Jesus said **John 14:30, "Hereafter I will not talk much with you: for the prince of this world cometh, and hath nothing in me.** Question, is Jesus dwelling on the inside of you? If you have Jesus, you have life times two, whom is head of all principalities and powers, the controller, authorized and pleasing to His Father God. Eyes tearing for no reason and never happened before, negative thoughts during the exam about possible results, this is not of GOD. The bible states to the study to show yourself approved. Study the Word of God and study your material for your exam, pray and take your exam. You may have told someone you confide in that you are taking a test and pray for you. If you did this, before your exam, ask God to abort any evil intentions or prayers prayed contrary to the results you need on your exam. How to handle those you see you know but don't communicate with you before you take your exam. Be cordial but keep the Word of God flowing in your mind. Just as we study to show ourselves approved in the Word of God, study for exams for school which most of the time your income is being secured in which we only owe ten percent to the Lord and an offering. Even sometimes you are sitting taking your test and a demon has jumped in you and you didn't take your test and that's why you can't pass it. Just like

when a couple, a marriage between a man and a woman, one must state their name, you must tell this demon that I am "your name" I love God and I need God, and I would be nothing without God because if it wasn't for him I would be nothing. Tell the devil briefly during the test I am "your name" and God said, But seek ye first the Kingdom of God and his righteousness, and then all these other things shall be added. Tell the devil, His time is limited and the Word of God in **Isaiah 54:16 "and I have created the waster to destroy."**

Tell the devil, the God of Abraham, Isaac, and Jacob rebuke Him in the name of Jesus Christ. God told Moses to stretch forth his rod and the red sea parted and the Israelites were delivered from the Egyptians on dry land. Who would have thought that could be done. Tell the devil, The God of David during war that led him and guided him through strong enemies that the Lord rebuke my enemy, IN THE NAME OF JESUS CHRIST. Tell the devil, that the God of Elijah that provided him with shade and comfort through the tree and a raven providing food (**I Kings 17:1-9**), the Lord rebuke you in the name of Jesus Christ. Tell the devil, that no power exceeds the power of our LORD AND SAVIOR JESUS CHRIST. Tell the devil, none other name but the name of JESUS may be called and men receive SALVATION. Tell the devil, NO WEAPON formed against me shall prosper, because I am a believer in our LORD AND SAVIOUR JESUS CHRIST. It could be one that bought the book to help you or sat with you to help you study without your knowledge it was part of a slow sudden death. If you could see who was sitting beside you, never wanted you to pass or their spiritual leader, or wickedness through the school. But, good news. God is still on the throne ruling and His eyes are not closed, and God is certainly not afraid of anyone and best of all he has never lost a battle. God never stopped fighting for His people in the Old Testament, and in the New Testament sent His only begotton Son, Jesus to suffer for you to receive Salvation and Life more abundantly.

God's way
There were many people in programs that would have succeeded but the enemy used strategic forces to halter their progress. I ask God for the ones that allowed the enemy to use them to accomplish this evil, that the evil will be returned to them and I forgive them in the name of Jesus Christ. I also ask and pray that God will restore the loss to the individuals if they so desire through them or their next generation in the name of Jesus Christ.

## Medical Yokes

You may have a physician that does not desire you to get well. You continue to see him and he places you on this plan for your health. Know when to change doctors. If you choose to keep those that you have, ask God to abort any evil desire on behalf of the medical or nursing staff, and most of all your family, that would lead to a undesired result on your behalf. Can a yoke attach itself to staff, nurses, medical staff, even those being educated in the medical field, the answer is yes. Know that Jesus is a yoke destroyer, brass breaker, and iron cutter not excluding any metals, materials, visible or invisible, known or unknown to man.

## Our Prayer

Father God in the name of Jesus, send your sharper than any two edged sword, Jesus Christ, through this yoke, originator of it, and the demonic forces working in it in the name of Jesus Christ. Lord, the Word of God states, But He was wounded for my transgressions, bruised for my iniquity, the chastisement of my peace was upon them and with His stripes, we are healed in the Mighty name of Jesus Christ. The Lord Rebuke you Satan in the name of Jesus Christ. **I Peter 2:24, "Who, His own self bare our sins in his own body on the tree, that we, being dead to sins, shall live unto righteousness, by whose stripes we are healed."** If you are not dead to sin, this would be the hindering factor. Submit yourself to God, resist the devil and he will flee from you. Being dead to sin is defined as being in fine tune with the

Word of God and the Holy Spirit. Being dead to sin means that the desires of a lifestyle not pleasing to God is not being fulfilled by you. In short, you have to put down the instruments that you received from satan, denounce him, and his works and have received and believed Jesus Christ and are now walking in the truth which is the Word of God, whom is Jesus Christ. **Allow everything we have to submit to you Lord and be kept in Jesus Name!**

## Visitor Yokes

You may have visitors coming to wish you well with their mouth and deep down in the crevices of their heart if they could without being seen would take your last breath. These visitors could be immediate family, previous coworkers, spiritual leaders, etc...You see them and you don't know who sent them. Did someone call them and tell them you were doing better or did the enemy feel the grip he had on you release. For example, your mother could be standing at your bedside but an evil force is with her. You began to dislike your mom not knowing it is the demonic force that was sent by another human that wants you gone. You may be on a bed of affliction but you need to pray too. Because the one watching you may become weary. The bible states in the garden of Gethsemane when Jesus went to pray and left the disciples to watch. He came back and found them sleeping. What if Jesus didn't pray for himself? Through the prayer Jesus prayed, God sent angels to strengthen him to endure the next course of events.

This does not mean they didn't love Jesus. Peter love was shown when the ear of the enemy was cut off. But Jesus let him know this was not a physical fight, but it is a spiritual battle. In the midst of him just previously praying in the garden asking God to remove the bitter cup, then being strengthened by the angels, took the ear of the soldier and performed another procedure, surgery, miracle in the garden without a stitch, consent for surgery, and no anesthetics or indication after procedure that there ever was an injury. Jesus just picked up his ear and placed it back, didn't say follow-up with me in a few days at the cross. The soldier had already received the cross experience, being touched by the holy hands of the SAVIOR OF THE WORLD whose pure hands touched no doubt some of his blood purifying him also during the surgery purifying the soldier. A Man of God once stated when the crown of thorns were placed on the head of Jesus, redemption was already taking place. Jesus said in the Word of God, God sent not His Son into the world to condemn the world, but that the world through Him might be saved (John 3:17).

A sitter may be assigned and the sitter does not know God and a demonic force was launched to watch in your care. Pray for the Lord to cover the sitter, too. It's not a good thing when a spiritual leader is ready for your demise and is praying for you and is somewhat aiding or hurrying the process.

I have visited many sick and shut in and no matter the level the illness. I prayed for God to heal them. God gives life and He knows our final date. You may be lying on a bed of affliction and the doctors from a medical standpoint have given you the time frame of your life. Remember, man didn't give life. God made the man, Adam and blew the breath of life in him and made him a living soul. Is it right when you are afflicted that through some demonic channel try to take the strength of the well. The bible states that "God girds me with strength" Stay in the word and stop doing wrong this can cause your prayers not to be answered. If you're weak for a little while, just maybe God intended this for you to rest, read, and meditate on the Word of God day and night and now maybe you'll be like that tree that's planted by the rivers of water that bringeth forth fruit in his season. Pray and ask God to gird you with His strength and believe the Word the God.

## Associate, Bachelor, Masters, Doctorate Yokes

Remember on an airplane there may be first class. They call for those needing assistance, military, first class, and those members of airplane miles program.

Those needing assistance? Are your receiving disability because you can't work or were to taught how to answer questions to the examiner to receive the disability. For example, you go on the plane first and everyone sees you and maybe have pity because of your need for assistance but we must all realize God knows the heart during the whole process. Are you able to work, actually this would probably be mentally beneficial to many. Instead of being upset knowing someone receiving it knowing that they faked it. Ask God to pull the cover, have them reevaluated, or better yet, they want to be disabled. I ask God to restore one truly disabled person for every one faker and allow the faker to be truly disabled and fully restore the truly disabled that God would receive the Glory of the testimony. Some of these disabled, you sit with in the House of God, they see you trying to work and still come to church, bible study, and they want to launch forces to cause you havoc. Just maybe this will shift their mind into another arena. Praise the Lord!

Don't sit behind first class, jealous and upset because you cannot afford to sit up there. Many are financially able to sit in first class but choose not to pay the difference. Question? Are you on the plane? The destination of the plane has not changed. If you're flying from Houston to Charlotte, everyone on the flight will land in Charlotte. If you really want to sit up there, pray and ask God to make this happen for you one day. The pilot is in place. It is good that he is flying the plane but you don't know whether He knows who made the sky he is flying in. Or whether he believes in the first, second, and third heaven. Or whether he realizes the plane that he is flying, God made the hands of the man and helped with the invention of the plane. He may be the pilot but God is above him.

Paul was on a ship stated in the Word of God that went through currents in the water I believe would not be withstood normally. Paul during this ship ride was not free physically. Paul could have focused on his problems during this ship ride, shipwreck, but an angel sent by God let Paul know that no one on the ship would perish. When told this, he was no way near the shore. He instructed the people to eat. They just obeyed, did he tell them that they would need this strength to make it to shore. The boat broke apart, but everyone that was on the boat made it to shore. God is real. Do you know who He is? If the Word of God said it, believe it, trust in it, quote it, stand on it, sleep with it, breath it, ride with it, hold it, lift it up, speak it, meditate on it, see it, read it, know it, study it, and hide it in your heart.

Paul was prisoner on the ship and Paul told the centurion, a man of authority that commands thousands of people. This attitude could have been on the ship, who are you, I am in charge, you don't tell me what to do, I am over thousands and they all have to do as I say. The centurion believed the words of the owner of the ship opposed to the Words of Paul. Paul stated in the Word of God, Sirs, I perceive that this voyage will be with hurt and much damage, not only of the landing and ship, but also of our lives. The ocean didn't obey him, the Word of God stated they were told not to go a certain place in the sea, but they would not listen. But I praise God for the record that the sea and winds obeyed Jesus Christ. The Word of God states in **Matthew 8:27, "But the men marveled saying, What manner of man is this that even the winds and sea obey him!"** This is whom I serve on today and everyday, Jesus Christ. Therefore if Jesus Christ is dwelling on the inside of me, which is where it pleased the Father that the fulness dwells and I am lining up with the Word of God, the seas and winds would obey me as well. The centurion and the owner (man) made the decisions and were in charge of the ship but now they were no longer in control, the ocean and winds was in charge as stated in the Word of God "we let her drive." The word of God states that there was neither sun nor stars in many days appeared, and no small tempest lay on us, all hope that we should be saved was then taken away. Now the centurion and the owner of the ship needed God, Paul already knew Him. God is still on the throne. Now the prisoner not on man's payroll but God's payroll is about to be in charge of the ship.

The angel didn't speak to the centurion or the owner but to the prisoner, Paul was listening for the Word from the Lord. Physically, the workers wanted to make sure the undergirding of the ship was secure for the currents, but spiritually make sure your spiritual foundation is firm, just as Jesus said to Peter in **Matthew 16:18 "upon this rock I will build my church and the gates of hell shall not prevail against it."** No matter your physical location, make sure you are standing on the rock, Jesus Christ and He dwells inside of you. Paul's foundation was Jesus Christ, he was fasting, and not stated, but I believe in constant prayer to the Lord. Paul, the prisoner gave the report of what would become of the ship and lives. The people may have not known but on the ship, Paul had them on a fourteen day fast and then instructed them on the day they reached the shore to eat. They needed food the last day for energy and strength to swim to shore and praise God, just as Paul stated, no lives were lost.

Your friend has a master's degree and you have Bachelors. Or maybe you attempted your Master's and received your degree. Now this yoke that you are better than me sent to my head through a demonic force and I should look at you as being above me. I have a degree(s) and you have a degree(s). Remember your degree will not eliminate any questions at judgment but you will have more to answer. Some people have come to you for help and some had the resources to help but somehow was turned away. You may have received your degree after you aided in wickedness to ensure someone else not complete the program. And now you feel since you have obtained your degree everything is great and your sins are without punishment. The devil is a liar. I ask God to repay this evil to you through a loved one or immediate family, or better yet make some restrictions on your goals and things you are trying to pursue. God is still on the throne. You have all these degrees you want read out that you have most through wicked channels hurt people that had good intentions to help. A mentor of mine once stated, "You cannot help everybody, not just one man" but Jesus can help everyone. God knows the heart, if your intentions are to destroy the vessel, God knows when they need to go. I ask God to repay the evil. This is not good when you are sent or asked to go somewhere, and maybe God sent you a place to help in an area and you were railroaded, turned away, or evil forces were launched for your demise. It's what you want. I abort the evil forces of the enemy in the NAME OF JESUS. I ask God, just as the Word of God states he would take a stony heart and make it into a heart of flesh. I ask God to drop a holy stone on the evil, wicked, stony heart and grind it into powder. Then let God know you will praise him in the dust/powder for his goodness, and because He is God whom answers prayers.

## Yokes Preventing The Word of God From Going Forth
This yoke is to make a pastor/one in leadership to substitute word time with other things. There is no substitute for the Word of God. Bible study is bible study. The definition of bible study is to meditate, ponder, and discuss spiritually, receive spiritual instruction and application of the WORD OF GOD. Some people are going through and the enemy will use who he can to get you off track. Again a pastor should be able to identity this demonic force unless he/she is part of plan. Just remember, an account will be given by the pastor, all those in positions, non-members, participants, and all other workers of iniquity in that day known by God. During the sermon very little word but mostly, talking about other things some which may be beneficial and some not is not acceptable.

Praise the Lord! During a hurricane crisis the people need to know that **thrice (three times) Paul suffered but withstood Perils of "shipwreck" noted in II Corinthians 11:25.** Therefore if you have Jesus Christ you too can withstand the hurricane. Praise the Lord!

## Passing the Baton
Do you have the kill the next person to receive baton or should the person kill the person they just got it from. When running in the Olympics, one team with many members must run a certain distance and then pass the baton to the next runner. The goal is the finish line. If teamwork is aborted and discord

manifests in any part of the team or plan designed the chances of winning is decreased. The goal of each team and member of the team should be to run per distance set for each player and to pass the baton without dropping it to the next runner until the finish line is reached without much loss of speed during transfer. If the passing of the baton is premature on the receiver end and the holder of the baton is still is able to function effectively in the role this is great. But what if some demonic forces has been launched to compromise his ability to lead in his role.

Ask God to expose the enemy and his devices. Ask God to protect the one receiving injury from these forces and to restore him back. This is your choice for this next prayer. You could ask God not to allow the person to ever be able to hold the position ever or better yet it is between you and God. Just don't hate the one that did it, Word of God states to love everybody. How can I expect God to answer my prayer when I hate you? Most importantly speak healing of your body back to your desired functional level. Sometimes God will allow us to go through things so we can depend more on him. God wants to know you need him. Just as a husband as the Word of God speaks between a man and a woman. The man wants to know that you need him. Eve needed Adam and also Adam needed Eve but the man is the head...this is another book. Make sure there is no hatred in your heart. Ask God to search it even in places unknown or some known, but all areas where discussions are unlikely. Discuss it with God but go to him in humility and reference to the true and living God that brought forth water from a rock. The Israelites stood their needing water but knew it would come from God but didn't know how he was going to do it. So now you have the Rock, Jesus Christ and a physical rock and you need some water. The Word of God states, but my God shall supply all your need according to his riches in glory through Christ Jesus our Lord. Trust God. Man may say it cannot be done. I am too sick. Do you know what you have? The enemy will tell you to read the statistics of the disease. Educational information is good but the Word of God is above all that and we pray God will give you the cure for the problem you're suffering from. Healing is according to your faith. God holds life and death in His hands and your tongue, not your haters, or nonbelievers in your desired results. You hold the power of life and death in your tongue, therefore speak life regardless of how it looks according to **Proverbs 18:21, "Death and life are in the power of the tongue: and they that love it shall eat the fruit thereof."** Make sure you let God know when He heals your body you will testify of the goodness of the Lord and use the body that He has just restored to glorify Him. And that without the shedding of blood there will be no remission of sin and no healing.

The first shedding during His circumcision after birth. The shedding of blood also occurred when Jesus was pierced in His side, the shedding of blood occurred when the crown of thorns were placed on Jesus head and pressed, the shedding of the blood occurred as the stripes went to His back, some just showing superficial skin tears, lacerations, and deep wounds. The shedding of the blood occurred when a nail was placed in Jesus right hand to physically secure Him to the cross after He was lifted up, the shedding of the blood occurred when a nail was placed in Jesus left hand to physically secure Him to the cross, the shedding of blood occurred when a nail was placed in Jesus right foot, and the shedding of the blood occurred when a nail was placed in Jesus left foot. Jesus blood was shed when He was pierced in His side as stated in John 19:34 **"But one of the soldiers with a spear pierced his side, and forthwith came there out blood and water"** but you don't pierce Him by not believing, receiving, praising and serving Him, Jesus Christ resulting in your name not being in the Lamb's Book of Life in Jesus name (Revelations 1:7).**

Someone may ask, how can you pray these things. When you have known others to be accepted to a program of study, build homes, win money, receive advanced positions on a job, or any other good things and deep in your heart you've given them your best wishes. Sometimes even knowing you want to go but never doing anything to cause harm to another or even ill wishing they not receive their degree. This is how you can pray this. Especially when others whom hate you see you as prey, attempt to take your life by suicide, on the highway, snakebites and/or during your sleep. Just as doctor is aiding the baby to come out through the birth canal, the enemy is there sometimes attempting to assist you to your death if you let him. I have heard those in spiritual leadership say God told me to do this to you. If you have a Pastor in sin, how can they truly hear from God and know God's voice from the enemy's voice. If this has happened to you and you don't believe God desired for you to go through this, you could pray and ask God to return the evil to them and their family. God knows if it was warranted or not. Paul knew when the angel came and spoke the word, he didn't need a translator, and he knew God sent Him. Just as the parable in the bible states the owner of the vineyard sent last his son and they killed him too. When people know the Spirit of God dwells in you, believe me the devil knows. He can send a cobra to your face in the middle of the night and God is with you, divine protection. He will try to disturb your sleep so you may be drained of energy and sometimes through the unit, usually cool at night and you wake up hot, what's going on with my unit. It's the enemy, pray and know the difference. Your calling for the unit to be checked and the devil is behind it, service fee. He will come at you anyplace he can. I rebuke the enemy this day. God is still on the throne, you may be well today but I ask God to repay the evil to you in Jesus Name. I bind any retaliation of any demonic forces in the NAME OF JESUS, of this prayer even to those whom I didn't know was plotting against me, in Jesus Name.

Someone may feel because they are a certain race, they somehow are better than you. First you need to the let the devil know **Acts 17:26, "And hath made of one blood all nations of men for to dwell on all the face of the earth, and hath determined the times before appointed, and the bounds of their habitation."** The nations were together in one place speaking the same language but was building something in unity that God was not in agreement of. Therefore, the project was halted God changed man language that they could no longer work together with understanding. Make sure your project is being done that the name of the Lord will be glorified and you have His approval. Second let the devil know that what they were doing which was building tower in Babel to reach heaven and God stopped them by making different languages. Then let the devil know, we are all humans made by God and no matter the color or creed, we will all stand before the same judgment. There is a book called the Lamb's Book of Life and people may rule parts of the earth but they cannot rule the heavenly throne. **It was prophesized by Jacob in that "Ephraim would be greater than Manasseh" (Genesis 48:19-20).**

## Wicked Yokes of Hate

This yoke may occur because you refuse to release someone that you dislike for no reason or hate with cause. First we must address hate. God is love and every human being has a purpose. To intentionally try to destroy someone out of jealousy or hatred is not acceptable. You must ask the Lord to deal with your heart. Just like a smoker's lungs are black or discolored from years of smoking, the heart will began to constrict leading to high blood pressure, increase of pressure on the arteries, which will eventually effect every organ in the body system. Decreased renal function, decrease in endocrine function, etc..... Release the person, release the problem, release the situation, whatever it is and give it to God, whom knows all about man and knows how to settle it while you're trying to decipher it. Cast your care on Him for He careth for you.

## Prayer to Destroy the Spirit of Hate

Father God in the name of Jesus
Satan, the Lord rebuke you and the spirit of hate planted in the name of Jesus Christ. Lord you said in your Word that you will teach us those things we need. We need in the name of Jesus for you to teach those with hearts full of hate the beauty of loving each other just as you have loved mankind. Deal with each individual issue in the name of Jesus Christ that causes mistreatment and discord. Lord deal with the outside interference and yokes being placed in the home, workplace, place of worship, and all places

whose intent is to distract. The power of God and the power of Jesus Christ let me know, they exceed the enemy and his devices. I speak life and health and speak death of the hatred demons and devices of the adversary in the name of Jesus Christ. One must realize that the enemy end will be the Lake of Fire. I serve Jesus Christ and thank God for sending Him and appreciate all He has done and continues to do. Lord, you said in the Word of God the shield of Faith will quench every fiery dart of the enemy and we ask you Lord to allow the shield of faith to quench, block, abort, sever, and detonate the devices of the wicked in the name of Jesus Christ.

## Presidential Prayer 0701.14

Father God in the Name of Jesus Christ. Lord, we pray for the President of the Unites States. Lord Lift him up on every side in the name of Jesus. Brattle the wicked tongue and restrain the hand of deceitfully and openly wicked in the name of Jesus Christ. Expose the enemy and his devices. Deal with the wicked known and unknown in various parts of government and in the world in the name of Jesus Christ. Lord thank you for directing his paths as He holds in Honor the Highest Office of Government in the United States. Look on the first family and keep them on one accord and in alignment with you Lord in the name of Jesus Christ in that all scripture is still in the process of being fulfilled. Thank you for shielding them with the shield of faith in the name of Jesus and Lord we ask that they never put down the Sword of the Spirit which is the Word of God in the name of Jesus Christ. Lord we exalt you, praise you, bless you, adore you, honor you, glorify you, and give homage to your Holy name in the name of Jesus Christ. Lord we will continue to look to the hills whence comest our help, knowing all our help comes from you Lord. Lord, we look to you Lord, the supplier of all our needs according to your riches in glory. Lord, we look to you and bring our tithes, knowing you will open the windows of heaven and pour out blessings that we won't have room enough to receive while we continue to support the church in the name of Jesus Christ. Lord we ask the release of a Holy rolling stone faster than the speed of light to devour enemies visible and invisible in the name of Jesus Christ. Lord we thank you for divine protection through Jesus Christ in the name of Jesus Christ. Silence, muzzle, and restrain the visible enemy and the one's in sheep government clothing in the name of Jesus Christ. Great is the Lord and Greatly to the praised, for his greatness is unsearchable in the name of Jesus Christ. Lord we pray for peace in Israel in the name of Jesus Christ.

Thank you for lives and the examples of those who attended, served, and worshiped you in church services indeed with honor. Lord comfort those mourning in the name of Jesus Christ. Lord we ask in the name of Jesus Christ, just as many were watching and in tune with the World Cup that they will have this same eagerness about the things of God in the name of Jesus Christ. Lord we thank you for marriage between a man and woman. Lord we thank you for President Barack Obama and Michelle and their two children. Lord allow if possible for us to see more family interaction and church attendance in the name of Jesus Christ.

## Prayer For Those With Anxiety

Father God in the name of Jesus Christ. Lord we praise and exalt your Holy Name. We thank you for being our God and thank you for shedding your blood and dying on the cross for the remission of our sins and for healing in every area. Lord we are thankful that God raised you from the dead and you sit alive on the right hand of your Father, God. Lord there are some suffering with anxiety and other attacks because they have not received you or they have not fully trusted in you. Lord most would say they have Jesus, but the question is does Jesus have all of you. Which parts are you still trying to hold on to? Release everything to God to use, correct, rectify, and trust me when God gets finish you will be right. Lord we ask you look on the minds of those whom do not trust you and we ask you to increase their faith in you Lord in the name of Jesus Christ. Lord you said in **Proverbs 3:5-6, "Trust in the Lord with all thine heart and lean not to thine own understanding. In all thine ways acknowledge him and he shall direct your paths.** Father God in the name of Jesus, the Word of God states to "Be careful for nothing but in everything by prayer and supplication with thanksgiving to let your request be made known unto God." Lord you said to **"Pray without ceasing"** in I Thessalonians 5:17. **Job 22:28** said " **Thou shalt also decree a thing, and it shall be established unto thee: and the light shall shine upon thy ways"** because I am a servant of the Lord whose righteousness is of Him. Lord we ask you to suffocate the anxiety demonic forces in the name of Jesus Christ that they are no longer existent. Lord we are careful and we fear you Lord in the name of Jesus and we pray for Peace in Israel in the name of Jesus Christ. In prayer, praise, and exaltation to you Lord, we reverence you as our King of Kings, and Lord of Lords, we thank you in advance for answering our prayers in the name of Jesus Christ.

## Prayer For Those on Ventilators

Lord, strengthen the lungs of those on ventilators. Lord protect them from spirits of suffocation and lung constricting spirits in the name of Jesus. Lord if perhaps this was launched by one known to the patient that desires there demise, expose them in the name of Jesus Christ. Lord, patients that have been in many hospitals, nursing homes, other health care facilities and some happy for their progress and many not. Lord protect them the more from forces known and unknown in the name of Jesus Christ. Lord also deal with hospital wickedness in the name of Jesus Christ because the patient may have transferred from their facility. Every patient belonging with evil attached to it, I bind the forces unknown and known to me in the name of Jesus Christ that prevents their progress in the name of Jesus Christ. Those patients whom do not know you Lord, our prayer is for them to receive you Jesus and your precious blood, receive Salvation and healing in the name of Jesus Christ.

## Prayer for Israel in which the United States of America Love

Lord we thank you for Israel and Jerusalem. Lord we thank you for bringing peace back to Jerusalem. Lord we thank you for their President over Israel. Lord we understand in scripture, you told King Saul to kill all Amalekites and not to leave anything living and he killed some and brought the King and cattle back. The prophet met King Saul and had to complete the orders God gave King Saul. Lord allow the President in Office to do your will without compromise in the name of Jesus. King Saul ended up dying by the hands of an Amalekite and his two sons died also. My prayer is for peace and that the President/King of Israel will hear the pure voice of God through the Holy Spirit and follow his complete instructions in the name of Jesus Christ. Jesus is the King of the Jews and we thank God Salvation was extended to the Gentiles in whom everyone whom is not a Jew is.

## Prayer for Binding Wickedness at Large

Jesus, Head of all powers, Jesus, Head of all principalities, Jesus, Head of man, Jesus, Holder of all power in heaven and in earth.

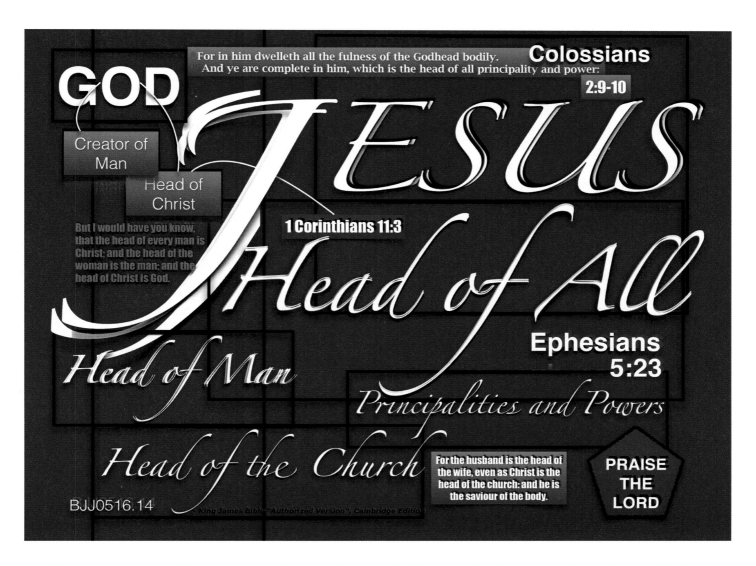

We ask you in your Mighty name to loose the bands of wickedness in the name of Jesus Christ. I believe through my spiritual eyes that the bands are loosening and coming undone in the name of Jesus Christ. I believe through faith that all other unknown and known attacks, agenda's have received the Stone that I have received in the name of Jesus Christ. I believe the iron, brass, metal, and all other unknown materials are broken, cut with the sharper than any two edged sword, Jesus Christ, and are now in pieces and nonfunctional permanently in the name of Jesus Christ. Lord we exalt you, praise you, adore you, honor you, thank you, give homage to your name, reverence you, and praise God for the Word of God **in Revelations 4:11, "Thou art worthy of all the honour, glory and power for thou hast created all things for thy pleasure they are and were created.** Lord we thank you for defeating hell, death, and the grave by the precious blood of Jesus, being shed on Calvary's Cross and power of your resurrection. Lord thank you that the fulness dwells in you and it pleased the Father, God.

## Prayer for the Conversion of Atheist and All Other Religions Whom Do Not Believe in God, to Jesus Christ in the Name of Jesus Christ.

Lord I pray for those just given an ultimatum to change from Christianity to another religion that does not serve Jesus Christ. My prayer that you will soften the hearts of the enemy and cause them to be converted to Christianity or Serving Jesus Christ in the name of Jesus Christ. Lord we pray that none of the Christians during this time will denounce God, Jesus, or the Holy Spirit. They will stand just as firm as Shadrach, Meshach, and Abednego knowing their God, the God of Abraham, Isaac, and Jacob, in whom we serve will deliver them in the name of Jesus Christ. Lord, *John 14:6,* **Jesus saith unto him, I am the way, the truth, and the life: no man cometh unto the Father, but by me.**

Father we ask you to open the hearts and minds of these unbelievers that they will believe and receive the Word of God. Lord we ask for over fifty percent of these will convert and receive salvation in the name of Jesus Christ. That they will now use their mouths to speak of you and hands to serve you in the name of Jesus Christ. They will testify that they were once unbelievers but now have believed and received Jesus Christ, and now praising and glorifying Him in the name of Jesus Christ. Open up their understanding in your Word in the name of Jesus Christ. Lord allow them to be ready for your return being holy in the name of Jesus Christ.

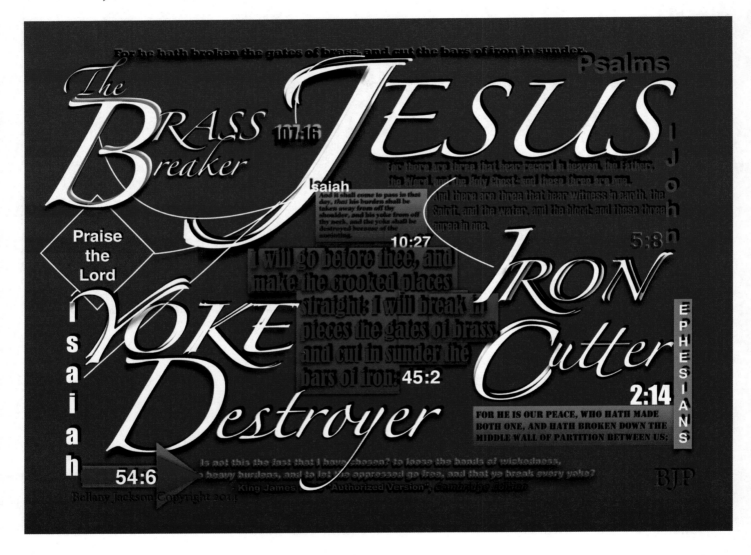

Most important point to know is that Jesus Christ is the head of all principalities and powers, given all power in heaven and in earth and it pleased GOD, whom made the heavens and earth and man from the dust of the ground, that the fulness dwells in Him, Jesus the head of man and head of the church. Know that Jesus is "Far above all principality, and power, and might, and dominion, and every name that is named, not only in this world, but also in that which is to come" Ephesian 1:21. "While ye have light, believe in the light, that ye may be the children of light" John 12:36a. Allow Jesus, the healer, redeemer, forgiver, strong-tower, stronghold, provider, sustainer, helper, guide, strengthener, shield, butler, my song, my salvation, my rock, brass breaker, iron cutter, yoke destroyer, burden lifter, reliever of the oppressed, wicked band loosener, and the door heal you in all areas those known and unknown to you in Jesus Name.

## Jesus, The Most Planned Pregnancy
**By Bellany Jackson**

JESUS, THE MOST PLANNED PREGNANCY[1]
WAS PERFORMED BY GOD
[2]THE CREATOR OF THE WORLD
AND ALL LIFE[3]
HE KNEW BEFORE THE FOUNDATION
OF THE WORLD HE SPOKE INTO EXISTENCE
THAT HE WOULD SEND HIS ONLY BEGOTTON SON[4]
WHOSE NAME IS ABOVE ALL NAMES[5]
AT WHOSE NAME DEMONS TREMBLE AND BELIEVE[6]
AT WHOSE NAME EVERY KNEE WILL BOW[7][8]
EVEN THE EGYPTIANS WILL SERVE JESUS CHRIST
WHEN THE SEPTRE IS REMOVED[9]
THIS SAME EGYPT WHERE THE SON OF GOD
WENT FOR SAFETY FROM KING HEROD[10]
SHORTLY AFTER HIS BIRTH, JESUS
AT WHOSE NAME SALVATION, REDEMPTION, ARE OBTAINED[11]
JESUS THE MOST PLANNED PREGNANCY BY GOD
KNEW WHO, WHAT, WHEN, WHERE, HOW, AND WHY
THE PURPOSE OF THE SAVIOR WAS KNOWN
BUT OLD TESTAMENT LIVES HAD TO WAIT
UNTIL THE FULNESS OF TIME HAD COME[12]
WHEN GOD ALLOWED THE HOLY SPIRIT
TO OVERSHADOW HER, MARY
CREATING BABY IMMANUEL IN THE FLESH[13]
THE CONCEIVED SAVIOR OF THE WORLD[14]
THAT IS JESUS, TO BRING REDEMPTION TO THE WORLD
WHERE JESUS WAS CARRIED IN UTERO[15]

---

[1] Luke 2:16, 2:7, 2:12
[2] Genesis 1:1
[3] John 1:3
[4] John 3:16
[5] Philippians 2:9
[6] James 2:19
[7] Romans 14:11
[8] Philippians 2:10
[9] Zechariah 10:11-12
[10] Matthew 2:13
[11] Romans 10:9-13
[12] Galatians 4:4
[13] John 1:14, I Timothy 3:16
[14] Matthew 1:20
[15] Luke 1:39 - 47

WHERE JESUS WAS HELD AND TRANSPORTED FOR SAFETY
WHERE JESUS WALKED
HEALING, DELIVERING, SETTING FREE
OPENING BLINDED EYES, MAKING THE LAME WALK[16]
CLEANSING LEPERS, RELEIVING FEVER[17][18]
TURNING WATER INTO WINE, DRYING UP CONTINUOUS FLOWS
ALLOWING HER TO RECEIVE
THE LIVING WATER NOW FLOWING OUT OF HER BELLY
JESUS FORGIVING SINS[19]
MAKING DISBELIEVING SOULS
BELIEVER'S IN JESUS CHRIST
RAISING A DEAD MAN FOR DAYS, LAZARUS [20]
ALIVE, EATING, LIVED, AND DIED AGAIN
BUT JESUS THE FIRST BORN FROM THE DEAD
NEVER TO DIE AGAIN
ALIVE ON THE RIGHT HAND OF THE FATHER
JESUS SITS
HEAD OF ALL PRINCIPALITIES AND POWER
HEAD OF MAN, HEAD OF THE CHURCH[21]
SETTING THE CAPTIVES FREE
UNDOING HEAVY BURDENS
LOOSENING THE BANDS OF WICKEDNESS[22]
SETTING THE OPPRESSED FREE
BREAKING AND DESTROYING EVERY YOKE
CUTTING IRON[23]
BREAKING BRASS
PREACHING GOOD TIDINGS UNTO THE MEEK
PREACHING THE ACCEPTABLE YEAR OF THE LORD
BINDING UP THE BROKENHEARTED
PROCLAIMING LIBERTY TO THE CAPTIVES
OPENING OF THE PRISON[24]
TO THEM THAT ARE BOUND
TO SET AT LIBERTY THEM THAT ARE BRUISED
JESUS WHOM THE SPIRIT
OF THE LORD WAS UPON
ANOINTED WITH THE HOLY GHOST
AND WITH POWER
WHO WENT ABOUT DOING GOOD
HEALING ALL

---

[16] Luke 7:22
[17] Matthew 8:14-15
[18] John 4:45-54
[19] Hebrews 9:11 - 10:29
[20] John 11:9-45
[21] Ephesians 1:20-2:22
[22] Isaiah 58:6
[23] Psalms 107:16
[24] Isaiah 61:1

THAT WERE OPPRESSED OF THE DEVIL[25]
FOR GOD WAS WITH HIM
JESUS, IMMANUEL, GOD WITH US
A MAN APPROVED BY GOD
AS EVIDENCED BY
MIRACLES AND WONDERS AND SIGNS[26]
WHICH GOD DID BY HIM, JESUS
IN THE MIDST OF YOU
PRAYFULLY DWELLING ON THE INSIDE OF YOU
THANK GOD FOR THIS PLANNED PREGNANCY
PRAISE GOD FOR THIS PLANNED PREGNANCY
EXALT YE THE LORD YOUR GOD[27]
AND WORSHIP AT HIS FOOTSTOOL
FOR HE IS HOLY
PRAISE GOD
WHERE JESUS CARRIED THE CROSS
WHEN JESUS WAS LIFTED UP[28]
WHEN JESUS WAS TAKEN DOWN
WHERE JESUS WAS PLACED
HOW JESUS ENTERED
THE HEART OF THE EARTH
THREE DAYS AND THREE NIGHTS[29]
GOD, RAISING JESUS FIRST FROM THE DEAD[30]
THEN OTHERS
A FAITHFUL GOD[31][32][33][34]
JESUS A FAITHFUL SERVANT
THE WORDS OF THE LORD[35]
ARE PURE WORDS
ALL PROVEN, REFINED LIKE JESUS
IN THE FURNACE OF THE EARTH
AS SILVER TRIED SEVEN TIMES
STAY RIGHT SO YOU WILL RISE TOO

BY BELLANY JACKSON
WRITTEN 0128-29.2015
Praise the Lord!

---

[25] Acts 10:38
[26] Acts 8:12-13
[27] Psalms 99:5
[28] John 12:32
[29] Matthew 12:40
[30] Revelation 1:5
[31] II Thessalonians 3:3
[32] I Corinthians 1:9
[33] I Corinthians 10:13
[34] I John 1:9
[35] Psalms 12:6

"Church of Jesus Christ,
The Head of All Principalities and Power &
Head of All Power in Heaven and in Earth"
&
The "Hear Jesus Network"
By
Pastor Bellany Jackson 0208.2015

All scripture is given by inspiration of God, and is profitable for doctrine, for reproof, for correction, for instruction in righteousness: (II Timothy 3:16) There is something to learn from every scripture in the Word of God!

**An example of giving your pearls to the swine**

King Ahaz gave a portion of the pearls of Judah from the House of God and Kings Quarter to King of Assyria while seeking ungodly counsel in which he did not receive the help solicited. Did King Ahaz know what he really was entrusted with or was he so far out in sin that he was blind? Jesus came to open the blinded eyes **(Isaiah 42:7, John 9:7-26, Luke 4:18)**.

When the distressed King Ahaz, who did evil in the eyesight of God, took silver and gold and precious possessions out of the House of the True and Living God and Kings quarters and gave them to the King of Assyria whom worshipped Idols and not the God of Abraham, Isaac, and Jacob **(II Chronicles 28:8, 21)** while seeking ungodly counsel/help that he would not find from Assyria. King Ahaz caused an increase in sin, mourning **(Proverbs 29:2)**, and "made Israel naked"**(II Chronicles 28:19)** but God notified them through Prophet Isaiah that the righteous Savior was soon to come **(Isaiah 7:14)** Jesus Christ, my Savior.

**I Peter 2:22 Who did no sin, neither was guile found in his mouth:**

**I Peter 2:24 Who his own self bare our sins in his own body on the tree, that we, being dead to sins, should live unto righteousness: by whose stripes ye were healed.**

**II Corinthians 5:21 For he hath made him to be sin for us, who knew no sin; that we might be made the righteousness of God in him.**

**I Corinthians 1:29-31 That no flesh should glory in his presence. But of him are ye in Christ Jesus, who of God is made unto us wisdom, and righteousness, and sanctification, and redemption: That, according as it is written, He that glorifeth, let him glory in the Lord.**

Look to God for the miracle, our Creator.

Seven Be's of the Lesson
_____

1. **Be Found Seeking Godly Counsel**

   **Psalms 1:1 Blessed is the man that walketh not in the counsel of the ungodly, nor standeth in the way of sinners, nor sitteth in the seat of the scornful. But his delight is in the law of the Lord; and in his law doth he meditate day and night)** (Seek God First by Bellany Jackson)

2. Be Found Seeking, Worshipping, Drawing Nigh, and Praising the True and Living God and Jesus Christ, the only Begotton Son of God and Be Found in the Book of Life (http://youtu.be/oTbyt7y-jQO)

   Matthew 6:33, "But seek ye first the kingdom of God, and his righteousness; and all these things shall be added unto you."

   Revelations 4:11, "Thou art worthy, O Lord, to receive glory and honor and power: for thou hast created all things, and for thy pleasure they are and were created."

   James 4:8, "Draw nigh to God, and he will draw nigh to you. Cleanse your hands, ye sinners; and purify your hearts, ye double minded."

   Psalms 150: 1-6, "Praise ye the Lord. Praise God in the sanctuary: Praise him in the firmament of his power. Praise him for his mighty acts: Praise him according to his excellent greatness. Praise him with the sound of the trumpet: Praise him with the psaltery and harp. Praise him with the timbrel and dance: praise him with stringed instruments and organs. Praise him upon the loud cymbals: praise him upon the high sounding cymbals. Let every thing that hath breath praise the Lord. Praise ye the Lord."

3. Be Found doing Good in the Eyesight of the Lord whom Sees All

   I Peter 3:10-13, "For he that will love life, and see good days, let him refrain his tongue from evil, and his lips that they speak no guile. Let him eschew evil, and do good; let him seek peace, and ensue it. For the eyes of the Lord are over the righteous, and his ears are open unto their prayers: but the face of the Lord is against them that do evil."

   Hebrew 4:12, "For the word of God is quick, and powerful, and sharper than any twoedged sword, piercing even to the dividing asunder of soul and spirit, and of the joints and marrow, and is a discerner of the thoughts and intents of the heart." (Hail to Jesus My King by Bellany Jackson "DO YOU KNOW THE BRASS BREAKER, IRON CUTTER AND YOKE DESTROYER JESUS CHRIST ALBUM.")

4. Be Found not Giving Your Pearls to the Swine

   Matthew 7:6, "Give not that which is holy unto the dogs, neither cast ye your pearls before swine, lest they trample them under their feet, and turn again and rend you."

5. Be Found not increasing sins and causing nakedness among people

   I Peter 1:16, "Because it is written, Be ye holy; for I am holy."

   II Corinthians 10:3-6, "For though we walk in the flesh, we do not war after the flesh: (For the weapons of our warfare are not carnal, but mighty through God to the pulling down of strong holds;) Casting down imaginations, and every high thing that exalted itself against the knowledge of God, and bringing into captivity every thought to the obedience of Christ; And having in a readiness to revenge all disobedience, when your obedience is fulfilled."

   **Jesus Is the Resurrection I** by Bellany Jackson "DO YOU KNOW THE BRASS BREAKER, IRON CUTTER, AND YOKE DESTROYER JESUS CHRIST"

6. **Be Found Ready awaiting the return of Jesus Christ**

   **Matthew 24:44 Therefore** be ye also ready: for in such an hour as ye think not the Son of man cometh.

7. **Be Found not Giving an Enemy of God Precious Silver and Gold out of the House of God while seeking ungodly counsel**

(Jesus Holy, Heavy Steps by Bellany Jackson).
https://itunes.apple.com/us/album/do-you-know- brass-breaker/id925094879
(Jesus Dayspring by Bellany Jackson)

Copyright 2015 Bellany Jane Jackson Jaynebell77@icloud.com

# Thank God For Freedom

From One Blood Came Every Nation
The Americans Came to Transport the Africans
To The United States
Unwillingly We Came
Crying, Kicking, Screaming
Packed Tightly In Conditions I Will Not Mention
Placed in Bondage
When King Mannasseh Was Placed In Bondage
He Cried Out to God and God Changed Him
From A Sinner To A Believer In The Power Of God
With Evidence of Praise, Worship, and Complete Devotion To Him
We, African Americans Decades and Decades Ago
Were Placed In Bondage To Be Freed
Placed In Bondage For A Better Opportunity and Better Life by God
Placed In Bondage But Learned Much From The Americans
Placed In Bondage In Which Many Lost Their Lives
Placed In Bondage and Mistreated
Leaning on The Savior, Jesus Christ
For Deliverance
Didn't Know Who, How, When, or Where It Would Come
Just As The Move Of the Holy Spirit
As Compared to The Blowing Of The Wind
Elisha Sprinkled A New Cruse with Salt In the Barren Water
Made it fruitful, productive, even to this day
Elijah Smote the Jordan River
The Water Parted and They Walked On Dry Ground
As He Was Taken Up In A Whirlwind
Elisha Smote The Jordan River
The River Closed Back To Normal
Jesus The Christ
Baptized In The Jordan River
God, The Father Spoke
This Is My Son In Whom I Am Well Pleased
When Those Bound Had Enough
Cried Out At The Riverside
Bus Experience, Martin Luther King Experience
Peaceful Protest While Openly Praying To The Almighty God
Thank God For the Sacrifice
Thank God For Freedom
We Are The Only People I Know That The Americans
Traveled The Distance To Transport
To America
Most Africans in The United States
Are No Longer 100% African
Because Mixtures Occurred
We Are African American By Name

But Also Most By Blood
What Change Were We Seeking
Equality, Freedom, Acceptance, Rights
Ability To Have The Same Opportunities of All Americans
Ability To Have Family, Children, Homes, Security, and Love For America
Ability To Worship, Honor, Praise, Adore, Exalt the Almighty God
While Giving Him Thanks For Sending His Only Begotton Son
Jesus The Christ
Now Since We Are Out Of Bondage

Let's Ensure The Voting Rights Bill Is Renewed
By Evidence of Votes Needed to Pass 400+
Without Delay
Jesus Christ Was Sent
To Loose The Bands of Wickedness
Set The Oppressed Free
Break Every Yoke
Undo Every Heavy Burdens
Break Brass
Cut Iron
Preach Deliverance To The Captives
Sent To Heal The Broken Hearted
Recovering Of Sight To The Blind
To Set At Liberty Them That Are Bruised
To Preach The Acceptable Year of the Lord
Lord We Ask In The Name Of Jesus
To Loose The Wicked Bands Remaining
Destroy the Yokes Remaining
Heal Broken Hearts
And Bind Up Their Wounds
Sever Iron
Shatter Brass
Which Is All Done In The Name Of Jesus Christ
Whom Is Head Of All Power and Principality
And I Believe This is All Done Now In Jesus Name
I Never Heard A Boat Sent Not Making It Back To The US
No Sinking, Shipwrecks, Malfunctions, etc...
Secure Transportation to A Destination
Of Hope, Purpose, Dreams To Be Fulfilled, Abundant Life
Desire No Lack and No Want In Jesus Name
Delight Yourself In The Lord
And I Will Give You The Desires Of Your Heart
A Blessing To See
A Man Whom Was Just In His Teens
During The Original Selma Experience
Introduce and Walk The Bridge
With The First Black President and First Lady Of The United States and Others
What A Mighty God We Serve

How God Perserved Even Them
From Dangers Seen and Invisible Which We Give God Praise
And Didn't Allow The Desire Of The Enemy Be Fulfilled
Praise The Lord
A Blessing To See The Historic Home
Where Many Interactions Occurred
With Government Through The Ministry Of Dr. Martin Luther King, Jr.
As a Child My Parents
Allowed Us To Tour In Atlanta Georgia While On Vacation
The Martin Luther King Center
In Which I Am Thankful and Grateful
And Honored To See The Beautiful Center In Place
In Honor Of A Man With Innumerable Sacrifices
For Us To Receive Freedom, Equality, and Justice

## CAN GOD FLY A PLANE
## YES WITHOUT ANY DOUBT
## THERE IS NOTHING HE CANNOT DO
## BY BELLANY JACKSON

WELL
GOD MADE HEAVEN AND EARTH
GOD MADE THE AIR WE BREATH
GOD MADE MAN FROM THE DUST OF THE GROUND
GOD GAVE MAN THE WISDOM TO MAKE THE PLANE
AND RESOURCES USED TO MAKE IT
GOD MADE THE AIRSPACE IN WHICH THE PLANE FLIES
GOD MADE THE GROUND IN WHICH THE PLANE LANDS
GOD MADE THE WASTER TO DESTROY
GOD KNOWS NOT ONLY HOW TO KEEP A PLANE IN THE SKY
BUT ALSO HOW TO ALLOW IT TO TAKE OFF AND LAND SAFELY
MAKE SURE YOU GIVE THE LORD THE PRAISE
BEFORE, DURING, AND AFTER THE FLIGHT
IN JESUS NAME

WE SEE THE HANDS OF GOD EVERYDAY
WHEN YOU SEE THE MOON
WHEN YOU SEE THE SUN
WHEN YOU SEE THE BEAUTIFUL OCEANS
WHEN YOU SEE ALL THE ANIMALS CREATED BY HIM
WHEN YOU SEE THE TREES AND SCRUBERY
BLOOMING PLANTS AND FLOWERS
WINDS BLOWING WHERE YOU CANNOT
FIND THE ORIGIN
GOD IS THE WIND
GOD'S MIGHTY HANDS ARE ALL OVER THE EARTH
CAN YOU SEE

GOD IS THE PLANE
THE VEHICLE WE ALL ARRIVED ON THIS EARTH
WE MOSTLY CAME BY BOAT
OVER A VAST BODY OF WATER
THEN ON LAND
TAKEN UNWILLINGLY
BROUGHT US HERE
ENSLAVED, AND YOKED IN BONDAGE
GOD
PROVIDED, MADE DOORS, OPENED DOORS
OPENED SCHOOLS, COLLEGES
OPENED AND FREED RIGHTS FOR OUR RACE
SECURED JOBS AND BROUGHT EQUALITY
FREED BY THE ALMIGHTY GOD
NO AREAS RESTRICTED
EVEN THE POSITION OF THE PRESIDENT
YES, THE PRESIDENT OF THE UNITED STATES
WHAT A MIGHTY GOD WE SERVE

TAKEN TO BE FREED
LET US REMEMBER ALL THE LIVES LOST
DURING THE FREEDOM EXPERIENCE
OF THE AFRICAN AMERICAN RACE

# References

*Matthew Henry Concordance online and book*

Cdbaby. (2014). Jackson, Bellany "Do You Know The Brass Breaker, Iron Cutter, and Yoke Destroyer Jesus Christ" Gospel Album. Retrieved @ http://www.cdbaby.com/cd/bellanyjackson1

Dake, Finis Jennings, *"Dake's Annotated Reference Bible; The Holy Bible Containing Old and New Testament of the Authorized or King James Version Text"* Georgia, Lawrenceville: Dake Bible Sales, Inc. 1989.

Huffington post: Health Benefits to Eggs. Updated 03/30/2013 (Retrieved 0805.2014) http://www.huffingtonpost.com/2013/03/30/health- benefits-of- eggs-yolks_n_2966554.html)

ITunes. (2014). Jackson, Bellany "Do You Know The Brass Breaker, Iron Cutter, and Yoke Destroyer Jesus Christ" Gospel Album. Published and Retrieved from https://itunes.apple.com/us/album/do-you-knowthebrassbreaker/id925094879

King James Bible Online. (2013-2015). *King James Bible "Authorized Version", Cambridge Edition.* Retrieved from 2013 to 2015 @ http://www.kingjamesbibleonline.org.

Mayo Clinic. (2014). Benign paroxysmal positional vertigo (BPPV). Retrieved online @ http://www.mayoclinic.org/diseases-conditions/vertigo/basics/symptoms/con-20028216.

Wikipedia: (2014-2015). Martin Luther King, Jr. Memorial. Last modified on January 19, 2015. Retrieved from http://en.wikipedia.org/wiki/Martin_Luther_King,_Jr._Memorial.

Wikipedia: President of the United States. Last modified on January 10, 2015. Retrieved @ http://en.wikipedia.org/wiki/President_of_the_United_States.

*White House. (2014).* Rosa Parks has a Permanent Place in the U.S. Capitol *retrieved* @ http://www.whitehouse.gov/blog/2013/02/27/rosa-parks-has-permanent-seat-us-capitol

Wikipedia. (2014-2015). Rosa Parks Memorial Building. Retrieved @ http://en.wikipedia.org/wiki/Rosa_Parks_Memorial_Building

YouTube. (2015,). Jesus World Cup by the "Hear Jesus Network." Published December 15, 2014. Retrieved from http://youtu.be/kHXojCbUPlY.

# About the Cover

## II Kings 2:19-21

[19] And the men of the city said unto Elisha, Behold, I pray thee, the situation of this city *is* pleasant, as my lord seeth: but the water *is* naught, and the ground barren.

[20] And he said, Bring me a new cruse, and put salt therein. And they brought *it* to him.

[21] And he went forth unto the spring of the waters, and cast the salt in there, and said, Thus saith the LORD, I have healed these waters; there shall not be from thence any more death or barren *land*.

[22] So the waters were healed unto this day, according to the saying of Elisha which he spake.

**This scripture is symbolic because God
later sent Jesus Christ to heal all the
waters, people, and
defeat death and barrenness.
Praise God for Jesus Christ!
Bellany Jackson**

## John 14:6

Jesus saith unto him, I am the way, the truth, and the life: no man cometh unto the Father, but by me.

## I Corinthians 15:26-28

[26] The last enemy *that* shall be destroyed *is* death.

[27] For he hath put all things under his feet. But when he saith all things are put under *him, it is* manifest that he is excepted, which did put all things under him.

[28] And when all things shall be subdued unto him, then shall the Son also himself be subject unto him that put all things under him, that God may be all in all.

Praise the Lord!

Printed in the United States
By Bookmasters